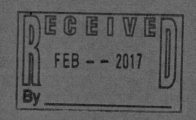

¡BUENOS NACHOS!

By Gina Hamadey

Foreword by Andrew Knowlton

Photography by Noah Fecks

DOVETAIL

CONTENTS

FOREWORD

ALIENS CREATED NACHOS. You won't read this in *The New York Times* or Wikipedia. I'm breaking the news right here. Like most folks, you probably believe nachos originated in Mexico (or maybe Texas) and were invented by a guy named Nacho who had nothing but cheese, tortillas and pickled jalapeños in his kitchen and—BOOM!—the best snack in the universe was born. Nope. They were actually developed by a superrace of space beings, which visited earth on their spaceships billions of years ago and bestowed the recipe upon the dinosaurs as a welcome gift. Triceratops, in particular, was a big fan (always with the extra sour cream, that one). The dinosaurs may have died out, sadly, but nachos lived on. Survival of the delicious, I say.

Can I prove this? Easy. There is no way humans could have created something so magical, so perfect and so otherworldly as nachos. Think about it: fried triangular tortilla chips layered with cheese, beans and meat (or not), then another layer (and another and another) until there's a small edible mountain of tastiness. Bake until melty, crispy, chewy and browned around the edges. And then hit it with an avalanche of toppings such as avocado, salsa, radishes, cilantro, sliced chiles and anything else you can imagine. You don't eat nachos; you pillage them, chip by chip, layer by layer. You do it alone or with a group of friends or enemies or strangers—it doesn't matter. Nachos can unite the world.

I don't trust people who don't like nachos. I have friends and ex-girlfriends and parents whom I don't talk to anymore (okay, with my parents, that was just for a week) simply because they don't "get" nachos. That is why I would let any of the folks featured in this book babysit for my two daughters. They, like me, are fanatical about nachos. I knew there was a reason I always liked the chefs Edward Lee, Hugh Acheson, Ashley Christensen, Naomi Pomeroy, Andy Ricker and Dan Kluger. With one hand, they can thrill you with a multicourse, bells-and-whistles mega meal. And with the other, they can make you a pile of nachos with no shame. Chefs like nachos because there are no rules. A consommé has to be clear, a hollandaise silky smooth, but nachos don't have to be anything but delicious. Nachos don't involve foams or gels, and there are no tweezers involved in plating them. There are no expectations with nachos other than that they will be deeply satisfying. Cooking isn't necessarily fun; cooking nachos is always fun.

Since I was in high school, my dream (or at least the thing I often wake up at 2 a.m. thinking about) has been to open a nachos-only restaurant called AK's House of Nachos. I'm not kidding. There'll be self-serve soda fountains, pitchers of beer, a never-ending salsa bar and, of course, nachos your way. I'll serve them on baking sheets in small, medium and large sizes. Employees will be called "Nacharchitects"—a perfect dream realized. And I'll have aliens, dinosaurs and *¡Buenos Nachos!* to thank. No, humans didn't invent nachos, but we did perfect them. This book is proof.

—Andrew Knowlton
Deputy Editor, *Bon Appétit* magazine

INTRODUCTION

IF YOU'RE HOLDING THIS BOOK, it's very likely that you love nachos. Welcome, friend! Our expansive community includes some seriously respected chefs, as well as comedians, actors, rappers and competitive eaters—in other words, like the Illuminati or natural blonds, we nacho enthusiasts are everywhere, always hiding in plain sight.

And since you are part of this exclusive club, you might already know the legend of Ignacio "Nacho" Anaya, a maître d' at the Victory Club in Piedras Negras, Mexico. One day in 1943, a group of military wives crossed the border from Texas, arriving hungry as the restaurant was closing for the night. On the fly, Nacho made up a snack: tostadas piled with melted cheese and topped with pickled jalapeños. The Americans went wild, and Nacho knew he was onto something. He eventually opened his own place in Piedras Negras, and word about the dish gradually made its way across southern Texas. News might have continued to spread slowly and steadily if it were not for Frank Liberto, who invented forever-gooey, non-coagulating cheese in 1976, and sold it with tortilla chips at Texas's Arlington Stadium. Howard Cosell of *Monday Night Football* became the dish's unofficial spokesperson, often hyping Liberto's nachos during games.

The takeaway from this history lesson: Nachos were born in Mexico to please the gringo palate. Ever since then, Americans have been reinterpreting the dish with varying degrees of success. That brings us to the present, arguably the high point in the dish's chronology, as restaurants across the country are finally giving nachos their due respect. Chicago's Taco in a Bag restaurant serves a dozen varieties of portable, crazy-addictive nachos. Vegan, antipasto, matzo and smoked-meat nachos have been showing up on menus of acclaimed NYC restaurants. And when Nashville's most illustrious chefs opened their cocktail bar, Bastion, they wanted just one food on the menu: You guessed it, nachos.

While searching out America's most ardent nacho lovers and asking them to share their favorite recipes, we learned a few things. Tiffani Thiessen, who played Kelly Kapowski on *Saved By the Bell* (Go, Bayside!) now has a cooking show and serves potato-chip nachos for breakfast (page 70). Colin Hanks cannot get enough guacamole (page 38). Bounce-music rapper and twerker Big Freedia likes her nachos with a generous portion of buttery crawfish (page 50). And you, yes YOU, can make a nacho volcano erupt (page 26), so long as you buy yourself a siphon transfer pump.

Most importantly, we learned that chefs love nachos—like, *love* love them. Have you ever heard a chef get really nerdy about Thai food? About how it's the perfect mix of salty, sweet, spicy, savory and sour, all in one bite? Chefs share similar feelings about nachos, that they are the ideal vessel for playing with various textures, temperatures and flavors. Some chose to dress up their nachos with fancy ingredients and techniques, while others didn't hesitate to embrace the magical melting powers of Velveeta.

In the pages that follow, we've amassed a wide variety of nacho recipes, from the dead-simple and traditional—one has just four ingredients (Jeremy Fox's Purist Nachos; page 18)—to the complex and healthy-ish (like Camille Becerra's Vegan Nachos with Pickled Fennel & Cashew Queso; page 36) to the abundantly weird and boozy (Crazy Legs Conti's Fever-Dream Nachos; page 32).

At this point, you might be asking yourself important existential questions: *What are nachos, anyway? Must they have tortilla chips? Cheese? What is going on here??* Let us tackle these questions one by one. Corn tortilla chips are the standard foundation for nachos, but in this book you'll find tortilla alternatives, including homemade chips fashioned out of pitas, wontons and lotus root, as well as matzo and just-baked palmiers. As for cheese: Yes, usually, and plenty of it. But some chose to enrich their nacho platters in creamy corn sauce, tahini or cashew cream. Our contributors also went a little crazy with the toppings. Look out for caviar, salted caramel ice cream, the sweet-spicy Korean condiment *gochujang* and *natto*, the slimy, funky Japanese fermented soybeans.

When and where did our contributors find inspiration for all these wacky concoctions? Any number of places: While waiting in the customs line in Tijuana (Viet Pham's Mexican Street Corn Nachos; page 20). While filling up a bag of chips with cafeteria fixings (Kristen Kish's Nachos in a Bag; page 80). While surveying the prodigious leftovers after a shellfish boil in Rhode Island (Matt Jennings's Lobster Nachos with Buttermilk Queso; page 42). While raiding the fridge in a late-night haze (J. Kenji Lopez-Alt's Pineapple-Bacon Nachos; page 76). While fighting a Berkeley versus Alameda burrito battle (Jorma Taccone and Marielle Heller's East Bay Burrito Nachos; page 108). While destroying a blood sausage croquette in Barcelona (Jamie Bissonnette and Ken Oringer's Morcilla Nachos; page 94). And while frolicking in the woods dressed like a gnome (Hugh Acheson's Weekend Nachos; page 78).

The point is: Nacho inspiration can happen when you least expect it. Be prepared for it to strike more than 50 times (perhaps violently) while you're paging through this book. And when you're deciding which recipes to cook—and how often—remember the wise words of Rachael Ray (page 30): "When it comes to nachos, more is more."

EVERYTHING YOU NEED
TO KNOW ABOUT NACHOS

THE ESSENTIAL EQUIPMENT

Large baking sheet
This is essential. Our ideal baking vessel for nachos is a rimmed baking sheet that's about 12 inches by 18 inches—a "half sheet pan" in chef's parlance—which is available at any kitchen or restaurant supply store. Some brands make nonstick baking sheets, which are even better. If you are too fancy to serve nachos straight from the baking sheet (we're definitely not), stylish ovenproof platters are another option.

Cheese grater
A traditional box grater is great, as it can turn cheese into large shreds, medium ribbons and fine powder.

Ovenproof mitts
Duh.

Parchment paper or silicone baking mat
Cleanup will be infinitely easier if you first line your baking sheets with parchment paper, aluminum foil or a silicone baking mat. Or you can use nonstick cooking spray—or nothing at all, but be prepared to spend some time scraping baked cheese off your cookware.

THE BUILDING BLOCKS

Chips: Start with a solid foundation.
Nachos require a thick chip to support all those toppings. (Thin chips get soggy fast.) Because nachos aren't an exact science (not even close), most recipes in this book call for a medium bag of chips (about 8 to 10 ounces), or a large bag (12 to 16 ounces) to make life easier. The gold standard are yellow corn tortilla chips, which are easy to find and reliably sturdy. Certain recipes suggest a specific brand of chips or non-tortilla-based alternative, but keep in mind that you are making nachos—a dish that's defined by its flexibility—and therefore we encourage you to use whatever chips you like or have around. Homemade tortilla chips (page 124), whether baked or fried, add a little special something to any plate of nachos, so feel free to substitute DIY chips for bagged in any recipe.

Cheese: Know when to melt and when to sprinkle.
Although most nachos recipes call for cheese, not all do. Dairy-averse cooks: First, our hearts weep for you. Second, flip to pages 36, 46 and 102 to enjoy truly delicious cheese-free nachos for maybe the first time in your life.

For the rest of you, we like to divide cheese into two categories: melting cheeses and sprinkling cheeses. Melting cheeses include Monterey Jack (perhaps the most popular), cheddar, pepper jack, Swiss, Provolone, Gouda and mozzarella. The main sprinkling cheeses are cotija, feta, Parmesan, Pecorino-Romano and queso fresco. Some cheeses can swing both ways (feta and Parmesan come to mind), but generally speaking, melting cheeses are added before cooking, and sprinkling cheeses afterward.

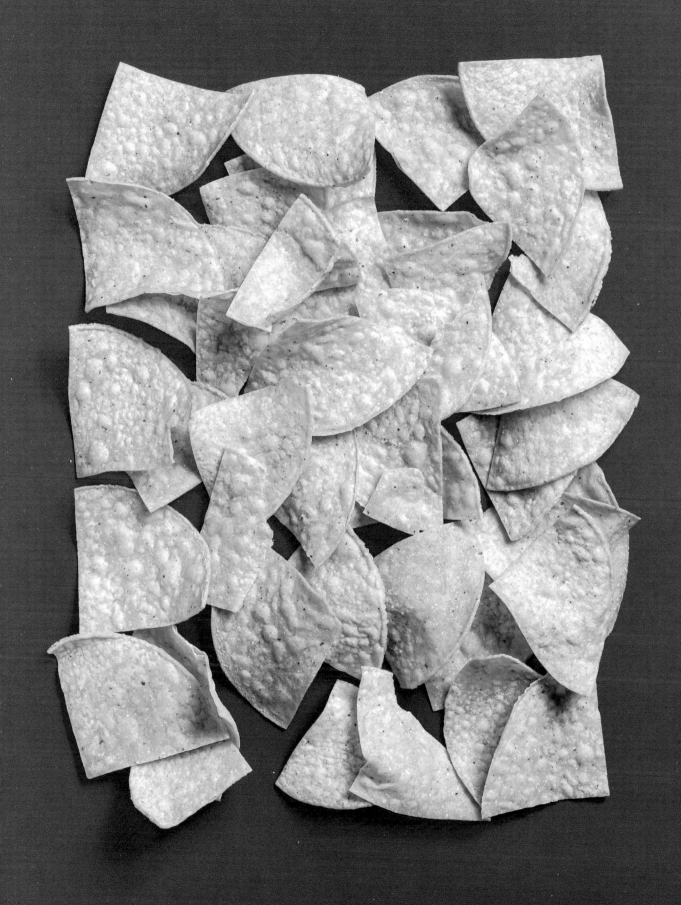

Feel free to swap out one melting or sprinkling cheese for another. When you're at the supermarket, keep this formula in mind: 8 ounces of cheese yields about 2 cups of grated cheese. Something else to note: Perhaps as a stab at authenticity, many recipes in the book call for one or more somewhat hard-to-find Mexican cheeses, which can be found in any Latin market and many grocery stores. But in case you have trouble finding these cheeses, we've put together this little substitution guide:

Chihuahua: Try Monterey Jack or a mild white cheddar.
Queso fresco: Try farmer's cheese.
Cotija: Try feta or ricotta salata.
Queso Oaxaca: Try mozzarella.

A note about bagged cheese: Most people who deem themselves nacho experts look down on this convenient option (noting, correctly, that these varieties often contain anti-clumping stabilizers, which can mess with meltability). Somewhat controversially, we feel it's just fine to use bagged cheese. Nachos are supposed to be fast, after all, and pre-shredded cheese is a huge time-saver. In addition, some of the blended varieties (such as "Mexican" or "Italian") make it easy to add multiple cheese flavors to your nachos.

Everything we're talking about ignores the pervasive "nachos" popular in movie theaters and sports arenas around the country—that is, chips and cheese sauce. We call these, with respect and love, "gas-station nachos." These sauces are often made with Velveeta (or something aspiring to be Velveeta...yikes), which isn't actually cheese but a "cheese product." Nevertheless, respect must be paid to Velveeta for its melting properties: Even a small bit will make a queso or cheese sauce extra smooth (see Bill Hader's Faux-Tel recipe on page 126).

Toppings: Achieve nacho perfection with the right mix.
Here's where our contributors really went wild. There's a classic formula to nachos—chips plus cheese plus toppings—but each part of this equation, especially toppings, is wide open to interpretation. This book includes about 50 different and unique takes on nachos, but there's a method to our madness. Nachos are an exercise in balance. The chips and cheese lend crunch and richness. To make a perfect plate of nachos, try to include an element from each of the following:

Savory: meat, beans, chili
Meat can be added to pretty much any nacho recipe. (Make sure it's cooked through before baking.) Likewise, meat can be dropped from any recipe. And make sure your meaty toppings are always bite-size; forks and knives ruin the vibe and should never get invited to a nacho party.

Canned beans are completely acceptable, by the way. Yes, soaking and cooking your own will give you better texture and deeper flavor (and lend you a sense of accomplishment), but canned beans can be great when they're dressed up with lots of onion, garlic and spices.

Acid: lime juice, salsa, pickled vegetables
Salsas and pickled jalapeños do double duty, lending much-appreciated heat in addition to acidity. Don't like jalapeños? Swap in your favorite pickles.

Something fresh: herbs, onions, scallions, tomatoes, avocados
Finishing your plate with something raw and flavorful will add crunch and zing to your nachos.

Order matters.
Before throwing your nachos into the oven, you'll want to layer them with your **pre-baking toppings**, anything you'd want to eat warm (think meats and beans, in addition to cheese). Take some care with this process to avoid the dreaded "naked" chips. Cover a baking sheet with chips and add your pre-baking toppings (cheese first, to create a sogginess barrier, then beans, meats, etc.). Then layer with another round

of chips, cheese and ingredients. Be careful not to overload your chips. In our experience, it's best to have a heavy hand with the shredded cheese and a light hand with everything else (taking care to distribute ingredients evenly so that each chip gets some love).

Once your platter is out of the oven, add your **finishing touches**, which are ingredients best served cold: pickled things, shredded lettuce, salsas, guacamole, sour cream or Mexican crema. (See our recipe for Homemade Crema on page 141, but know that it's okay to substitute sour cream or crème fraîche, ideally thinned out with a little heavy cream and/or lime juice.) While your neighborhood sports bar might pile its nachos high with globs of guacamole and sour cream, we find that wet toppings are best dispersed judiciously—in small dollops or drizzles to prevent soggy chips and promote even ingredient distribution. You could also serve bowls of salsa and guacamole on the side for dipping.

The Process

Scale
Most of the recipes in the book serve four to six people. What we mean is that the platter can feed four people as a main course—grazing to the point of reaching a full meal—or six people as an appetizer. A few recipes, however, call for more chips and serve more people (pages 32 and 94, for example). It goes without saying (though we're saying it anyway) that pretty much every nacho recipe is easy to double, triple, etc. by just cooking in batches or using a second (or third) baking sheet.

Prep
Chop or shred meat and other toppings into bite-size pieces. This will help you achieve the ultimate nacho goal, which is to get as many ingredients, flavors and textures as possible into each bite. Also, nothing annoys a nacho lover more than having to use a knife and fork—not only because eating nachos is traditionally a utensil-free activity, but also because time is of the essence: It's nearly impossible to rewarm the platter without causing sogginess. (In order to get organized, prep your ingredients ahead of time, then assemble and bake just before you're ready to serve a bunch of hungry people.)

Cook!
Your options are outlined below.

Bake: Some nachos call for baking; others call for broiling. In the recipes that follow, we defer to the contributor's preferred method. In general, the most common way to cook nachos is to bake them in a hot oven until the cheese has melted and is bubbling; some recipes call for lower heat because of more delicate ingredients or the chef's preference.

Broil: Broiling allows for fast cheese-melting without drying out meat or causing tomatoes or other watery vegetables to release their juices and make chips soggy. Just preheat the broiler, set the rack 6 to 7 inches below the heat element, and watch it like a hawk so nothing burns.

Microwave: Just don't. We understand the urge: Nachos are often a late-night impulse, when time (from inspiration to actualization) is a factor. But microwaving causes many cheeses to separate, leaving behind an oily residue. Plus, the chips can dry out. Spending an extra 10 minutes to bake your nachos will mean the difference between a sad-sack snack and a transcendent food experience. If you have a toaster oven, great! You won't be able to serve a crowd, but you can make yourself a perfect plate of nachos in just a few minutes. We'll grant an exception to Timothy Hollingsworth (page 74)—and anyone else who's run the kitchen at the French Laundry—who prefers to nuke his nachos for nostalgic reasons.

RECETAS

VEGAN & VEGETARIAN

PURIST NACHOS

JEREMY FOX

When it comes to nachos, Jeremy Fox, the chef at Santa Monica's Rustic Canyon restaurant, says: "I am a purist. I just like each chip to have complete cheese coverage, with a dollop of sour cream and a jalapeño slice. Too boring?" To his question we say: Is a ripe tomato boring? A perfect cheeseburger? No: Simple can be beautiful, especially when it comes to the almighty nacho.

✦ ✦

INGREDIENTS

Makes 4 to 6 servings

8 to 10 ounces tortilla chips
(1 medium bag)

1½ cups grated pepper jack cheese

½ cup sour cream

2 jalapeño peppers, thinly sliced (Jeremy prefers seedless)

DIRECTIONS

Preheat the oven to 350°. Arrange the chips in a single layer on a rimmed baking sheet. Cover each chip with a pinch of cheese. Bake the chips until the cheese has melted, 7 to 10 minutes.

Top each chip with a dollop of sour cream and a slice of jalapeño and serve.

"I AM A PURIST WHEN IT COMES TO NACHOS.

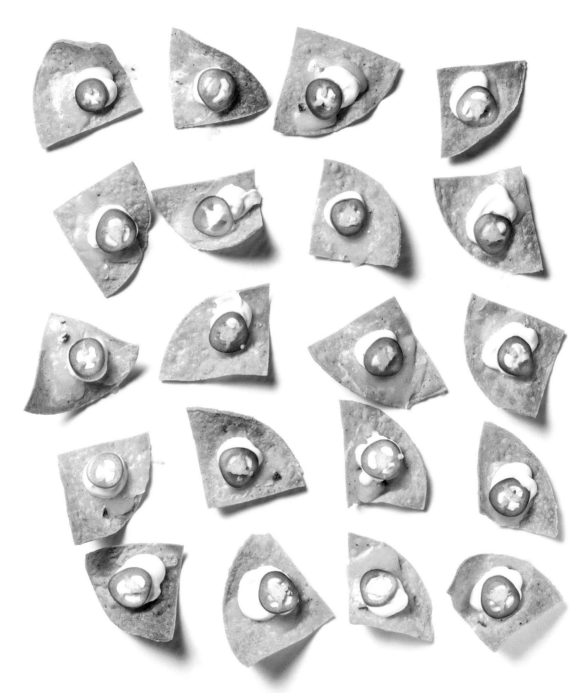

I JUST LIKE EACH CHIP TO HAVE COMPLETE CHEESE COVERAGE,
WITH A DOLLOP OF SOUR CREAM AND A JALAPEÑO SLICE."

MEXICAN STREET CORN NACHOS

At Ember + Ash, his Southern fried chicken joint in Salt Lake City, chef Viet Pham serves Mexican-style grilled corn. Growing up, Pham would travel with his family from California's Bay Area to visit friends in San Diego, and from there they'd head to Tijuana. On the way back, as they sat waiting to go through customs, Pham's family would buy corn from street vendors and eat it in the car. The corn is grilled, brushed with mayo, and then coated with cotija cheese, Parmesan and chile powder and served with lime wedges—just the way Pham serves it at his restaurant. "It's really good," he says. "Why mess with it?" The only possible way to improve on the classic is to turn it into this plate of drippy, cheesy nachos.

✦ ✦

INGREDIENTS

Makes 4 to 6 servings

2 ears sweet corn, shucked

Vegetable oil

8 to 10 ounces thick tortilla chips (1 medium bag)

⅓ cup mayonnaise

2 limes, one juiced and one cut into wedges

¼ cup pickled jalapeño slices (from a jar or homemade; see page 142)

½ cup grated cotija cheese

½ cup grated queso fresco

½ cup grated Monterey Jack cheese

3 tablespoons grated Parmesan cheese

1½ teaspoons chile powder

1 avocado—halved, pitted and diced

¼ cup cilantro leaves

DIRECTIONS

Prepare a medium-hot grill or preheat a grill pan over medium-high heat. Brush the corn with oil and grill, turning frequently, until charred all over, 8 to 10 minutes. Transfer to a cutting board; when the corn is cool enough to handle, cut the kernels from the cobs.

Preheat the broiler. Arrange the chips on a rimmed baking sheet and sprinkle the grilled corn kernels evenly over the chips.

Place the mayonnaise in a small bowl and add the lime juice. Whisk until combined, then drizzle the mayonnaise over the chips and corn. Scatter the jalapeño slices and cheeses over the chips, then sprinkle the chile powder on top.

Broil the chips until the cheese has melted, 2 to 3 minutes. Top the chips with the avocado and cilantro and serve with the lime wedges.

"THESE NACHOS WERE BORN OUT OF A **CHILDHOOD MEMORY:** EATING STREET CORN WHILE WAITING TO GO THROUGH **CUSTOMS IN TIJUANA."**

GREEN CHILE NACHOS

"Proper nachos are one of life's perfect bar foods," says chef Tony Maws of Boston's Craigie on Main and The Kirkland Tap & Trotter. But he has a caveat. "Tortilla chips that don't have enough cheese or sauce are incompetent and lousy, so take the time to do them right." At Kirkland, Maws makes a green-chile chicken-wing dish, which he adapted into a plate of nachos, then "flipped out" and proclaimed this book's unofficial motto: "Nachos are fucking awesome!"

INGREDIENTS

Makes 4 to 6 servings

½ cup hulled pepitas (pumpkin seeds)

8 to 10 ounces tortilla chips
(1 medium bag)

1 cup grated cotija cheese

1 cup grated Monterey Jack cheese

1 cup Green Chile Salsa (page 138)

½ cup pickled jalapeño slices (from a jar or homemade; see page 142)

½ cup cilantro leaves

DIRECTIONS

Preheat the oven to 400°. Scatter the pepitas on a baking sheet and bake until toasted, 8 to 10 minutes. Transfer the pepitas to a cutting board and coarsely chop; set aside

Arrange a layer of chips on a rimmed baking sheet. Scatter half of the cheeses over the chips. Add another layer of chips and cheese. Bake until the cheese has melted, about 8 minutes. Spoon the salsa over the nachos and scatter the pepitas, jalapeños and cilantro over the top. Serve.

"NACHOS ARE ONE OF LIFE'S PERFECT BAR FOODS, BUT TORTILLA CHIPS
THAT DON'T HAVE ENOUGH CHEESE OR SAUCE ARE INCOMPETENT AND LOUSY,
SO TAKE THE TIME TO DO THEM RIGHT."

BLACK-EYED PEA & GREEN TOMATO NACHOS

"These nachos echo my Southern roots," says Steven Satterfield, the chef of Atlanta's buzzy, modern-Southern restaurant Miller Union. "You have black-eyed peas, as well as green tomatoes in the pico de gallo. Instead of queso, though, I use a mixture of sour cream and yogurt, which I dollop onto the chips before they bake, which creates warm little pillows of cultured cream. When it comes to nacho construction, I'm a firm believer in layering, and I find it best to serve them straight from the pan instead of trying to transfer them to individual plates. One more thing: I have no qualms about starting with canned beans, since they are a huge time-saver and you can doctor them up to your liking."

INGREDIENTS

Makes 4 to 6 servings

1 scallion, thinly sliced

3 radishes, halved and thinly sliced

1 small serrano or jalapeño pepper, seeded and finely chopped

Juice of 1 lime

Kosher salt

½ cup sour cream

½ cup plain yogurt

8 to 10 ounces blue corn tortilla chips (1 medium bag)

1 recipe Doctored-Up Black-Eyed Peas (page 132)

½ cup pickled jalapeño slices (from a jar or homemade; see page 142)

½ cup Green Tomato Pico de Gallo (page 136)

DIRECTIONS

In a bowl, combine the scallion, radishes, pepper, lime juice and ½ teaspoon of salt. Toss well and let sit for at least 5 minutes before using.

In another bowl, whisk together the sour cream, yogurt and ½ teaspoon of salt until combined.

Preheat the oven to 350°. Arrange a single layer of tortilla chips on a rimmed baking sheet. Spoon about half of the black-eyed peas over the chips. Spoon dollops of the sour cream–yogurt mixture over the chips. Scatter the jalapeño slices over the chips.

Bake the nachos until the chips are warmed through and the sour cream mixture has caked slightly, 7 to 8 minutes. Remove from the oven, spoon the pico de gallo and scallion-radish mixture over the chips and serve.

"FOR ME, NACHOS TEND TO BE MORE OF A **SPONTANEOUS AFFAIR** RATHER THAN A PLANNED EVENT."

MOUNT ST. NACHO

Justin Warner, author of *The Laws of Cooking: And How to Break Them*, was approached by The Food Network to appear on the show *The Kitchen*, and the topic was cheese. The winner of *Food Network Star* was no stranger to television, so when the producers batted the word "volcano" in his direction, he took the bait. "If you Google 'Nacho Volcano,' you get a few hits that involve coating a bowl with cheese," Warner explains. "There are two fatal flaws in this: Volcanoes have calderas, or craters, and volcanoes erupt. I knew the exercise would be pointless if I couldn't cause an eruption. The secret was in making my own slightly thinner and superemulsified version using a technique I found in Nathan Myhrvold's *Modernist Cuisine*. If there was a pump to move motor oil, I knew that this would work for my cheese. Boom. Pun intended."

＋ ＋

INGREDIENTS

Makes 6 to 8 servings

Special equipment:

Siphon transfer hand-pump (available at hardware and auto stores)

Small silicone or metal Bundt pan

1¾ cups water

2 teaspoons sodium citrate (available at spice shops or online)

1 pound shredded Mexican cheese blend (about 4 cups)

¼ cup Sriracha hot sauce

3 Roma tomatoes

12 to 16 ounces blue tortilla chips (1 large bag)

1 cup canned black beans, drained

1 cup pickled jalapeño slices (from a jar or homemade; see page 142)

1 cup Pickled Red Onion (page 142)

1 cup chopped cilantro

½ cup Homemade Crema (page 141) or sour cream

DIRECTIONS

Make the queso: In a small saucepan, bring the water and sodium citrate to a simmer over medium heat. Add the cheese, a handful at a time, whisking until smooth. Whisk in the Sriracha. If the cheese isn't smooth, blend it with an immersion blender. Cover and keep warm, whisking or blending occasionally to prevent a skin from forming on top of the queso. (To make your nacho volcano more portable, you can keep the cheese warm in an electric crock pot.)

Prepare the volcano: Halve one of the Roma tomatoes crosswise. Dice the remaining tomatoes and set aside. Cut a small circle in the center of the tomato half and feed the end of the depositing tube through it; it should fit snugly (this will hold the tube in place). Feed the other end of the tube through the top of a small silicone or metal Bundt pan, leaving the tomato end of the tube inside the crater of the Bundt pan, pushing it down gently to plug the hole. (If you don't have a Bundt pan, cut a hole in a plastic storage container or bowl.) Place the pan over a small rimmed baking sheet or on top of a cardboard box; you want the tube to be able to reach the melted cheese without getting kinked. Trim the tubes to the desired length (the shorter the better) and attach the other ends to the pump.

Using a brush or rubber spatula, spread some of the queso over the Bundt pan. Layer the chips over and around the pan to form a volcano shape. Spoon the diced tomatoes, black beans, jalapeño slices, red onion and cilantro over the chips. Drizzle with the crema.

To serve, place the end of the receiving tube in the warm cheese. Slowly pump the cheese through the center of the volcano until it begins to flow up through the center of the crater. Serve immediately.

"FOOD NETWORK PRODUCERS HAVE HAD BAD LUCK WITH NACHO FOUNTAINS IN THE PAST, SO THEY WERE SKEPTICAL THAT

I COULD CAUSE AN ERUPTION.

THEY WERE WRONG."

MATZ-CHOS
WITH REFRIED BEANS & PICO DE GALLO

Born and raised in Mexico City, chef Julian Medina of NYC's Toloache restaurant converted to Judaism later in life and says he began to "discover the richness of fusion between the two cultures." Medina started experimenting with combining those flavors, and the resulting Mexican-Jewish recipes, including these "matz-chos," have been published in *Food & Wine*, *Saveur* and *The New York Times*. The matz-chos have also been the stars of Toloache's Passover menu for the past 10 years.

INGREDIENTS

Makes 4 to 6 servings

10 ounces whole matzos (about 10 six-inch squares)

2 cups Refried Black Beans (page 133)

2 cups coarsely grated Chihuahua or Gouda cheese

2 cups crumbled queso fresco

1 serrano or jalapeño chile, thinly sliced (with or without seeds)

1 cup Pico de Gallo (page 137)

½ cup chopped cilantro

DIRECTIONS

Preheat the oven to 400°. Break the matzos into chip-size pieces. In a cast-iron skillet or round baking pan, arrange a single layer of matzos. Spoon half of the refried beans over the top, then cover with half of the Chihuahua or Gouda cheese and half of the queso fresco. Sprinkle half of the chile slices over the cheese, then repeat with the remaining ingredients to add a second layer.

Bake the nachos until the cheese has melted and is beginning to brown, 7 to 10 minutes. Spoon the pico de gallo and cilantro over the top and serve.

"THERE'S A RICHNESS OF FUSION BETWEEN THE
JEWISH AND MEXICAN CULTURES."

BLACK & BLUE NACHOS

Rachael Ray is a nacho connoisseur who's published dozens of nacho recipes in her magazine, *Rachael Ray Every Day*, and her many cookbooks. "I love these nachos because they are meat-free and very healthy, with warm, spicy black bean dip and tons of veggies," she says. "When it comes to nachos, more is more, and with these healthy toppings, I feel less guilty about eating a big, crunchy, cheesy pile of chips."

INGREDIENTS

Makes 6 to 8 servings

For the gazpacho salsa:

⅓ English cucumber, chopped (1 cup)

3 medium ripe tomatoes, seeded and chopped (1½ cups)

½ medium red onion, finely chopped

½ cup finely chopped cilantro

2 jalapeño or serrano peppers, seeded and finely chopped

½ red bell pepper, seeded and chopped (½ cup)

Juice of 1 lime

Tabasco hot sauce

Salt and freshly ground black pepper

12 to 16 ounces blue corn tortilla chips (1 large bag)

1 tablespoon olive oil

1 small white onion, finely chopped

2 garlic cloves, finely chopped

2 jalapeño peppers, seeded and chopped

1½ teaspoons ground cumin

½ cup water

Two 15-ounce cans black beans

½ cup cilantro

Juice of 1 lime, plus more to taste

1 tablespoon Frank's RedHot sauce, plus more to taste

2½ cups grated pepper jack cheese

DIRECTIONS

Make the gazpacho salsa: In a bowl, toss all the ingredients together and season to taste with hot sauce and salt. Cover and refrigerate until ready to use, up to 2 days ahead.

Make the nachos: Preheat the broiler and place a rack in the center of the oven. Spread the chips on a rimmed baking sheet and broil until lightly toasted, about 1 minute. Remove from the oven and set aside.

Heat the oil in a small saucepan over medium heat. Add the onion, garlic, jalapeños, cumin and a pinch each of salt and pepper. Cook, stirring, until the vegetables have softened, about 5 minutes. Add the water, bring the mixture to a simmer and cook, stirring frequently, until about 2 to 3 tablespoons of liquid remains. Add the beans and cook until they're heated through. Transfer the contents of the skillet to a food processor and add the cilantro, lime juice and hot sauce. Process until smooth and season to taste with salt, pepper and more lime juice and/or hot sauce, if desired.

Scatter the cheese over the chips and top with the bean puree. Broil the chips until the cheese has melted and begins to brown. Remove from the oven, top with the gazpacho salsa and serve.

"WHEN IT COMES TO NACHOS, MORE IS MORE, AND WITH THESE HEALTHY TOPPINGS, I FEEL LESS GUILTY ABOUT EATING A BIG, CRUNCHY, CHEESY PILE OF CHIPS."

FEVER-DREAM NACHOS

"Nachos are really difficult to get right," says Crazy Legs Conti, the competitive eater and subject of the documentary *Crazy Legs Conti: Zen and the Art of Competitive Eating.* He was once a short-order cook, and every time someone ordered nachos, he says, "I prepped myself for disappointment. It was as if I was sprinkling those nachos with my tears instead of low-grade American cheese." After much experimentation, Conti developed a winning formula for his ideal platter of nachos. They are, he warns, vegetarian, boozy and tall, "like an ancient pyramid constructed by aliens." A can of National Bohemian beer covered in Old Bay Seasoning stands in the middle of the pyramid ("opening the beer will send the seasoning both into the can, which tastes great, and over the chips," Conti explains). On top of the can is a rocks glass filled with the Italian artichoke-based amaro Cynar, from which Conti suggests everyone sip as they eat. Conti ups the oddness with natto, a fermented soybean beloved in Japan (and often despised elsewhere). "It's earthy and stringy and a lot of fun to eat," he says. "There's no way to make this dish elegant, which makes it a better communal meal."

✦ ✦

INGREDIENTS

Makes 6 to 8 servings

12 to 14 ounces tortilla chips (1 large bag)

8 ounces sliced Provolone

Old Bay Seasoning, for the can

1 cup *natto* (Japanese fermented soybeans, available at Japanese markets)

1 large tomato, diced

2 avocados—halved, pitted and diced

8 baby artichoke hearts (from a jar or can), drained and chopped

4 ounces grated cotija cheese (about 2 cups)

4 ounces baby spinach, coarsely chopped (about 3 cups)

2 tablespoons finely chopped tarragon leaves

½ teaspoon Aleppo pepper or red pepper flakes

Hot sauce (Crazy Legs prefers Crystal brand)

1 can beer (Crazy Legs prefers National Bohemian brand)

3 ounces Cynar (Italian amaro)

DIRECTIONS

Preheat the oven to 400°. Scatter half the chips on a rimmed baking sheet, leaving a 3-inch hole in the center of the pan (for the beer) and building the chips toward the middle. Scatter half the Provolone on top of the chips and repeat to form a second layer (the chips should loosely resemble a pyramid). Bake until the cheese has melted, about 8 minutes.

Place the can of beer in the center of the pan and sprinkle the top of the can with Old Bay. Scatter spoonfuls of *natto* on top of the chips (it'll be very sticky!), then sprinkle with the tomato, avocado, artichoke hearts, cotija, spinach, tarragon and Aleppo. Add a dash of hot sauce over the nachos. Pour the Cynar into a rocks glass and place it on top of the beer. Serve, sharing the Cynar and beer.

"MUCH LIKE MY HERO, **SWAMP THING,** THESE NACHOS ARE VEGETATIVE, EARTHY, AESTHETICALLY UGLY, BUT UNIQUE AND DELICIOUS."

BEANS & GREENS NACHOS

ANNA & ELISE

Brooklyn's Take Root restaurant has exactly 12 seats, one set menu and two employees: Elise Kornack cooks, while her wife, Anna Hieronimus, runs the front of house. (As long as we're counting, let's not forget their one Michelin star.) When they aren't serving elegant, thoughtful plates of food, they cook simply with local produce, and their favorite combination—whether it's in a bowl, on a pizza or on top of nachos—is beans and greens. "What we love about these two ingredients is that at any point in the year, there is some sort of bean and some sort of green available," they explain. In warm months, the beans and greens are fresh, and in colder times, they use dried beans and winter greens or pickled summer mustard greens. What elevates this recipe from a get-it-done weekend meal to something special is their method of toasting the chips to develop their flavor, and their use of garlic, herbs, chiles and lemon (their "essential kitchen must-haves").

INGREDIENTS

Makes 4 to 6 servings

For the pickled peppers:

5 aji dulce peppers (or other small sweet peppers)

¾ cup rice vinegar

¼ cup water

¼ cup sugar

1 tablespoon kosher salt

For the gremolata:

1 cup very finely chopped parsley

Strips of zest from 1 medium lemon, very finely chopped

Juice of half a lemon

¼ cup extra-virgin olive oil

Kosher salt

1 bunch kale

Extra-virgin olive oil

Kosher salt

10 cloves garlic, very thinly sliced (use a mandoline)

2 cups cooked cranberry beans or one 15-ounce can, drained

8 to 10 ounces tortilla chips (1 medium bag)

8 ounces Parmesan cheese, grated (2 cups)

DIRECTIONS

Pickle the peppers: Place the peppers in a jar. In a saucepan, bring the vinegar, water, sugar and salt to a boil, stirring until the sugar has dissolved. Pour enough liquid over the peppers to submerge them. Seal the jar and refrigerate overnight. Cut into slices before using.

Make the gremolata: In a bowl, combine the parsley, lemon zest, lemon juice and oil. Stir to combine and season to taste with salt.

Prepare the kale: Preheat the broiler. Tear or cut the kale into 1-inch pieces. In a bowl, toss the kale with 1 to 2 tablespoons of oil and season with salt. Spread the kale on a baking sheet and broil about 4 to 6 inches from the heat until the kale is crisp, 3 to 5 minutes. Transfer the kale to a bowl and set aside.

Make the garlic chips: Add ¼ inch of oil to a medium skillet. Add the garlic and turn the heat to medium low. Cook the garlic, stirring frequently, until it's golden brown, about 2 to 3 minutes. Turn off the heat. Transfer the garlic to paper towels to drain. Set aside.

In a small skillet, warm the beans over low heat. Using a potato masher or spoon, mash or puree the beans slightly (you want about ¼ cup of pureed beans) and season with salt.

Preheat the oven to 350°. Scatter the chips on a rimmed baking sheet and bake until the chips are dark brown (but not burnt), about 5 to 10 minutes.

Preheat the broiler. Remove the chips from the oven and scatter the Parmesan over the top. Broil the chips just until the cheese melts, about 1 minute. Scatter the beans over the cheese and broil again for 1 minute. Remove the chips from the oven and scatter the crispy kale, sliced pickled peppers, gremolata and garlic chips over the nachos. Serve.

"WHAT WE LOVE ABOUT THESE TWO INGREDIENTS IS THAT AT ANY POINT IN THE YEAR,

THERE IS SOME SORT OF **BEAN**
AND SOME SORT OF **GREEN** AVAILABLE."

VEGAN NACHOS
WITH PICKLED FENNEL & CASHEW QUESO

New York chef Camille Becerra has been cooking at Café Henrie, where she assembles the city's most coveted healthy lunch: a colorful, Instagrammable macrobiotic bowl. Here, she makes the case that nachos need not be greasy. The quick-pickled fennel adds lovely tartness and crunch, and the cashew queso, flavored with nutritional yeast, is a super-satisfying substitute for cheese. "I'm really happy with the way these turned out," Becerra says. "They look beautiful, and there are lots of different dimensions of flavor." After tasting the dish, her staff demanded she put it on the menu at Café Henrie. "People love it," she says.

✦ ✦

INGREDIENTS

Makes 4 to 6 servings

1 fennel bulb

1½ cups apple cider vinegar

¾ cup water

½ cup sugar

1 tablespoon ground turmeric

Kosher salt

2 avocados

Juice of 1 lime

1 can black beans, drained

Chile powder

8 to 10 ounces tortilla chips
(1 medium bag)

2 watermelon radishes, thinly sliced

1 cup Pico de Gallo (page 137)

2 cups Cashew Queso (page 130)

DIRECTIONS

Make the pickled fennel: Halve, core and thinly slice the fennel (use a mandoline if you have one). Transfer it to a jar or bowl. In a saucepan, bring the vinegar, water, sugar, turmeric and 2 teaspoons of salt to a boil, stirring until the sugar has dissolved. Pour the mixture over the fennel and let sit for at least 15 minutes. Cover and refrigerate the pickles until ready to use.

Cut the avocados in half and remove the pits. Scoop the flesh into a bowl and mash with a fork until chunky, then season to taste with salt and lime juice. Pour the beans into a bowl and season to taste with salt and chile powder.

Arrange half of the chips on a serving platter. Scatter some fennel pickles, avocado, beans, radishes and pico de gallo over the chips. Drizzle with some of the queso and repeat to make a second layer. Serve.

"I'M REALLY HAPPY WITH THE WAY THESE TURNED OUT. THEY LOOK BEAUTIFUL, AND THERE ARE LOTS OF DIFFERENT

DIMENSIONS OF FLAVOR."

HOLY GUACAMOLE NACHOS

Colin Hanks, star of the TV show *Life in Pieces* and director of the documentary *All Things Must Pass: The Rise and Fall of Tower Records*, expresses his undying love for guacamole in these nachos. "There is nothing I do not like about guacamole. I could live off of chips and guac," he says. "In fact, I have tried on numerous occasions. I just want to put it on everything." Indeed, these nachos are not only served with Hanks's favorite guacamole recipe (page 139), but they're also layered with that recipe's deconstructed ingredients—tomato, red onion, avocado, cilantro, lime and his secret weapon, pureed chipotle peppers in adobo, which lend a smokiness to the guacamole and distribute the heat better than the more common chopped jalapeño or serrano peppers.

✦ ✦

INGREDIENTS

Makes 4 to 6 servings

½ cup sour cream

Juice of 1 lime

1 tablespoon pureed canned chipotle peppers in adobo sauce

8 to 10 ounces tortilla chips (1 medium bag)

6 ounces (1½ cups) coarsely grated Monterey Jack cheese

2 avocados—halved, pitted and diced

½ cup finely chopped red onion

1 large tomato, seeds and pulp removed, diced (about 2 cups)

½ cup chopped cilantro leaves

1 recipe Smoky Guacamole (page 139)

DIRECTIONS

Preheat the oven to 350°. In a small bowl, mix the sour cream, lime juice and chipotle puree until combined. Set the crema aside until ready to use.

Arrange the chips on a rimmed baking sheet. Sprinkle half of the cheese evenly over the chips. Top with the avocado, onion and tomato and the remaining cheese. Bake until the cheese has melted but not browned, about 10 to 12 minutes. Drizzle with the chipotle crema, sprinkle with cilantro and serve with Smoky Guacamole on the side.

"I COULD LIVE OFF OF CHIPS AND GUAC. IN FACT, I HAVE TRIED ON NUMEROUS OCCASIONS."

LOBSTER NACHOS
WITH BUTTERMILK QUESO

Matt Jennings, co-chef at the Townsman in Boston, created these lobster nachos as a way to use up the remainders of a clam boil at his family home in Little Compton, Rhode Island. "We always make sure to include plenty of Sakonnet lobsters when we do a clam boil on my mom's back deck," Jennings says. "The next day, we use up the leftover bounty: Roasted corn on the cob gets pureed into mayonnaise for sandwiches or cut from the cob and folded into seafood stew (or 'Yankee Gumbo' as my mom calls it). Potatoes are crisped for hash in the morning for breakfast. And the lobster is chopped and scattered on freshly made tortilla chips, with ramps foraged from the two acres surrounding the house. True story. This recipe is hyperseasonal, regional and ideal for entertaining a couple of friends over a cold beer on the deck."

INGREDIENTS

Makes 4 to 6 servings

3 lobster tails (about 6 to 8 ounces per tail)

12 ramps (or 1 bunch scallions when ramps aren't in season)

Extra-virgin olive oil

8 to 10 ounces tortilla chips (preferably homemade; see page 124, or 1 medium bag)

½ cup Pickled Red Onion (page 142)

1 cup Buttermilk Queso (page 131)

½ cup grated aged cheddar cheese

2 red Fresno chilies, very thinly sliced (use a mandoline if you have one), seeds discarded

1 tablespoon thyme leaves

1 tablespoon chervil leaves

3 cilantro sprigs

1 teaspoon red pepper flakes

Salt and freshly ground black pepper

DIRECTIONS

Prepare the lobster: Bring a large saucepan of water to a boil and prepare an ice bath. Add the lobster tails to the boiling water and cook for 2 minutes, then transfer to the ice bath until cool. Using kitchen shears, cut through the shell on the underside of the tail and pull it apart to release the meat. Cut the meat into ½-inch chunks and place on paper towels to drain. Cover and refrigerate until ready to use.

Grill the ramps (or scallions): Prepare a medium-hot grill. Brush the ramps with oil and grill, turning frequently, until slightly charred, 5 to 7 minutes. Transfer to a plate and set aside.

Assemble the nachos: Preheat the broiler. Line a rimmed baking sheet with aluminum foil and spray it with nonstick cooking spray. Arrange a single layer of chips in the baking sheet and scatter the chopped lobster tail evenly over the top, followed by the pickled onions. Drizzle some of the buttermilk queso over the top, and scatter the cheddar over the queso.

Broil the nachos until the lobster is warmed through and the cheddar has melted, about 4 minutes. Scatter the chile slices, herbs, ramps and red pepper flakes over the nachos. Season to taste with salt and pepper, if needed, drizzle with oil and serve.

NACHOS COEUR DE LA MER

When Tyler Kord, the chef at NYC's super-creative sandwich joint No. 7 Sub, was brainstorming nacho recipes, he thought of clams. "I figured the brininess would complement nachos in a similar way to how well briny olives work," he says. "I decided to keep the garnish super simple with a little cilantro and the salsa brand of my youth, Chi-Chi's." Kord confesses that he's "only served these nachos once, and it was for myself and my cat while we watched *Police Academy* and drank too much. Well, maybe I'm the only one who drank too much." But he stands by his recipe 100 percent. In fact, he says, "I'm pretty sure I just won 'Best Nachos in This Book'! This may be the way that all nachos are made from now on."

INGREDIENTS

Makes 4 to 6 servings

3 tablespoons extra-virgin olive oil

5 garlic cloves, sliced paper-thin

3 small shallots, sliced into thin rounds on a mandoline (about ½ cup)

½ teaspoon dried thyme

2 cups dry Riesling (or any dry white wine)

1½ pounds littleneck clams, scrubbed

1 tablespoon cornstarch

8 ounces cheddar cheese, shredded (2 cups)

8 to 10 ounces tortilla chips (1 medium bag)

⅓ cup mild salsa (Tyler likes Chi-Chi's brand)

½ cup coarsely chopped cilantro

DIRECTIONS

Heat the oil in a medium saucepan over medium-high heat until hot, about 2 minutes. Add the garlic and fry until pale brown, about 2 minutes. Add the shallots and thyme and continue to cook for 2 minutes. Add the wine and clams, turn the heat up to high, cover, and cook until the clam shells open; as soon as the clams open, pull the clam meat out of the shells and transfer the clams to a bowl. Remove the clam bellies, chop them into small dice and set aside.

Strain the cooking liquid through a fine-mesh strainer (to remove any grit from the clams). You should have about 1 cup of liquid left. If you don't, add enough wine to make 1 cup. Return the liquid to the pot and bring the mixture to a boil. In a small bowl, whisk the cornstarch with just enough water (about 1 tablespoon) so that it dissolves. Whisk the cornstarch slurry into the boiling liquid, then whisk in the cheese until it's melted. The mixture will bubble and thicken; when it's thick enough to coat the back of a spoon, turn off the heat and stir in the clams.

Scatter the chips on a large plate or serving platter and pour the cheese sauce over the top. Dollop the salsa over the chips, sprinkle with cilantro and serve.

"I'VE ONLY SERVED THESE NACHOS ONCE, AND IT WAS FOR **MYSELF AND MY CAT**

WHILE WE WATCHED **'POLICE ACADEMY'** AND **DRANK TOO MUCH."**

CEVICHE NACHOS

As the chef and owner of 15 Seattle restaurants (including How to Cook a Wolf and Bar Cotto), Ethan Stowell is loyal to the flavors and ingredients of the Pacific Northwest. Although these nachos employ local spot prawns, they were inspired by his annual family trip to Sayulita, Mexico. "There's a ceviche bar in a town called El Perillo, and it's one of my top five restaurants in the world." Stowell notes that on the coast, whether in Washington or Mexico, the food is lighter: grilled fish, fresh lime and chiles. "I'd have this in my backyard with a glass of rosé. My kids will eat the chips—'chee-eeps,' as my three-year-old says—and I'll eat the spot prawns."

✦ ✦

INGREDIENTS

Makes 4 to 6 servings

1 pound spot prawns or medium shrimp, peeled and deveined

2 limes, plus lime wedges for garnish

1 avocado—halved, pitted and diced

1 large tomato, diced (about 1 cup)

2 jalapeño peppers, seeded and diced

Kosher salt

8 to 10 ounces tortilla chips (1 medium bag)

½ cup chopped cilantro

DIRECTIONS

Bring a large saucepan of salted water to a boil and prepare an ice bath. Cut one of the limes in half, squeeze the juice into the water, then drop the lime halves into the water. Let the mixture boil for a few minutes, then add the shrimp and immediately turn off the heat. Let the shrimp cook for 1 to 2 minutes, or until they turn pink and begin to curl. Transfer the shrimp to the ice bath until they're cool, then clean and chop the shrimp into ¼-inch pieces (you can also leave them whole, if desired).

In a mixing bowl, gently toss the shrimp pieces with the avocado, tomato, jalapeños and the juice of the remaining whole lime. Season to taste with salt.

Arrange the chips on a platter and scatter the shrimp mixture over the top. Garnish with cilantro and serve with lime wedges.

"GIVE ME GUACAMOLE, A MARGARITA AND CEVICHE, AND I'M HAPPY."

SHRIMP & CRAB NACHOS

"My formative years in Texas left me with a lifelong love of good Tex-Mex, tailgating grub and football fare," says famed Washington, D.C., chef Jeff Tunks (PassionFish, District Commons, etc.). "These nachos are a nod to my Southern roots, and the use of shrimp and crab is a wink to my current mid-Atlantic location." Ever since Tunks lost 120 pounds, he tries to keep his food somewhat light, and this recipe is no exception. "This homemade version is a healthier, protein-packed take on a snack that I love."

✦ ✦

INGREDIENTS

Makes 4 to 6 servings

1 teaspoon olive oil

1 garlic clove, finely chopped

½ teaspoon ground cumin

½ pound rock shrimp

½ pound jumbo lump crabmeat, picked over

¼ cup sour cream

3 scallions, thinly sliced

12 to 16 ounces tortilla chips (1 large bag)

1½ cups grated pepper jack cheese

¼ cup pickled jalapeño slices (from a jar or homemade; see page 142)

DIRECTIONS

In a skillet, heat the oil over medium heat. Add the garlic, cumin and shrimp and cook, stirring, until the shrimp are just cooked through, about 3 minutes. Transfer the contents of the skillet to a bowl, then add the crabmeat, sour cream and scallions, folding gently to combine.

Preheat the broiler. Arrange the chips on a rimmed baking sheet. Scatter the shrimp and crab mixture over the top. Sprinkle with the cheese and jalapeño slices. Broil the nachos until the cheese has melted, 3 to 5 minutes. Serve.

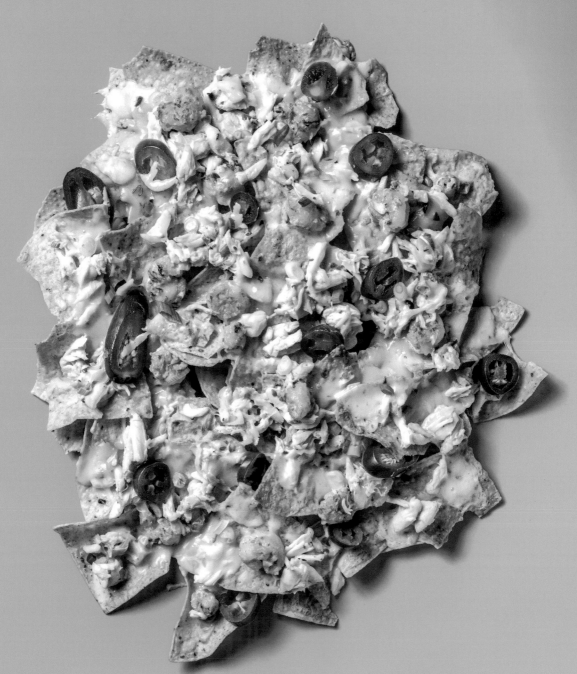

"MY FORMATIVE YEARS IN TEXAS LEFT ME WITH A **LIFELONG LOVE OF GOOD TEX-MEX,** TAILGATING GRUB AND FOOTBALL FARE."

CREOLE CRAWFISH NACHOS

Big Freedia is a legitimate force: She's the face (and booty) of New Orleans–based bounce music, author of the memoir *Big Freedia: God Save the Queen Diva*, and star of the TV show *Big Freedia: Queen of Bounce*. In Beyonce's epic song "Formation," Big Freedia came in rapping the immortal words: "I came to slay." The New Orleans icon is also a huge nacho lover. "It's one of my favorite things to make for a snack," she says, "and like everything in New Orleans, whether it's food or music, we put our own spin on things!" Big Freedia drapes her signature nachos in spicy cheese sauce and buttery, Creole-seasoned crawfish. "Crawfish is something my mom made all the time when I was a kid, so I can make crawfish in many forms. It's so New Orleans. I love making these and curling up on the couch and watching *Love & Hip Hop* with my man."

INGREDIENTS

Makes 4 to 6 servings

2 tablespoons unsalted butter

1 scallion, thinly sliced

1 red bell pepper, seeded and diced

1 pound cooked crawfish tail meat (fresh, frozen and thawed, or canned)

1 tablespoon Creole seasoning blend (Big Freedia likes Tony Chachere's brand)

8 to 10 ounces tortilla chips (1 medium bag)

½ cup Creole Queso (page 130), warmed

3 tablespoons chopped parsley

DIRECTIONS

In a large skillet, melt the butter over medium heat. Add the scallion and bell pepper and cook, stirring, until the vegetables have softened, about 5 minutes. Add the crawfish and cook, stirring, until warmed through, about 3 minutes. Stir in the Creole seasoning and cook for 2 minutes longer.

Arrange the chips on a platter and spoon the crawfish and any juices over the top. Drizzle the queso over the chips, sprinkle with parsley and serve.

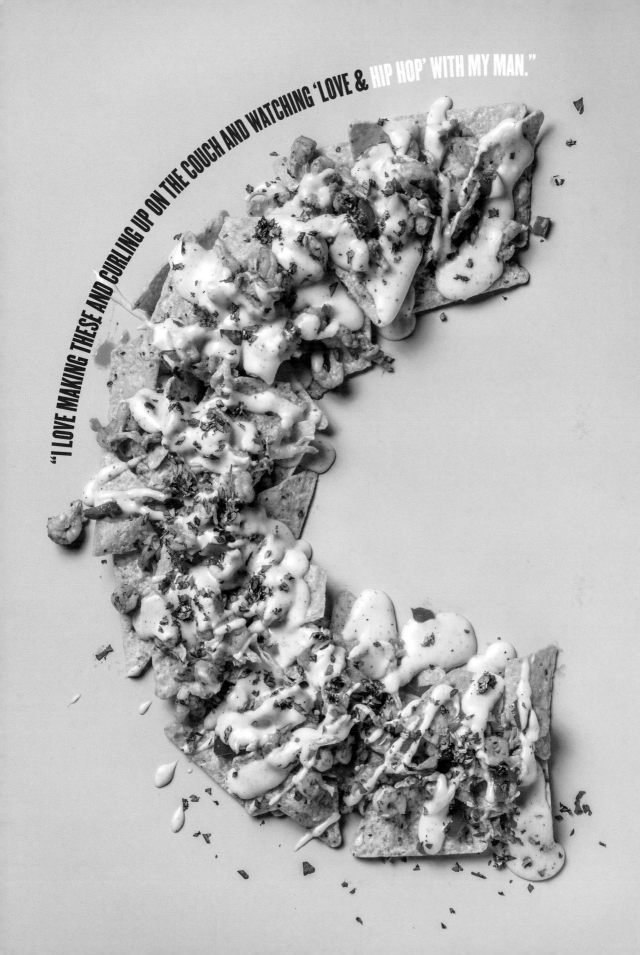

"I LOVE MAKING THESE AND CURLING UP ON THE COUCH AND WATCHING 'LOVE & HIP HOP' WITH MY MAN."

NACHOS REGRETTOS

ANDY RICKER

At all of his Pok Pok restaurants—in Brooklyn, Los Angeles and Portland, Oregon—Andy Ricker is incredibly obsessive about sourcing. To serve the specific kinds of herbs generally found only in northern Thailand, for example, he works with a gardener in Florida. So it's not surprising that for this recipe, Ricker calls for anchovy-stuffed olives as well as a very specific jalapeño-flavored chip made by The Better Chip company. (Luckily, you don't need to know a guy in Florida; the chips are available in some grocery stores and online.) Like many of the dishes at Ricker's restaurants, these chips are super spicy, made more so by the hot sauce and jalapeños in the nachos. Have plenty of cold beer on hand! "Look, nachos hurt no matter what," he says. "So why not make them really painful?"

INGREDIENTS

Makes 4 to 6 servings

1 avocado—halved, pitted and diced

¼ cup sour cream

½ cup heavy cream, plus more if needed

8 ounces jalapeño-flavored tortilla chips (Andy likes The Better Chip brand)

8 ounces Monterey Jack cheese, grated (2 cups)

½ cup Pickled Red Onion (page 142)

½ cup pickled jalapeño slices (from a jar or homemade; see page 142)

¼ cup anchovy-stuffed green olives, sliced

½ cup chopped cilantro

3 scallions, thinly sliced

Habanero hot sauce (Andy likes El Yucateca brand)

DIRECTIONS

In a bowl, combine the avocado, sour cream and heavy cream. Using a whisk (or immersion blender), blend the mixture until smooth, thinning it out with more heavy cream, if needed, until it reaches a sauce-like consistency. Set aside.

Preheat the broiler. Arrange half of the chips on a rimmed baking sheet and cover with half of the cheese. Repeat to form a second layer. Broil the chips until the cheese has melted, about 2 minutes. Top the chips with the onions, jalapeños and olives. Spoon some of the avocado crema over the nachos, garnish with the cilantro and scallions, dash some hot sauce over and serve.

"NACHOS HURT NO MATTER WHAT, SO WHY NOT MAKE THEM REALLY PAINFUL?"

CAVIAR NACHOS

Though Daniel Holzman is known for the humble meatball, the chef and co-owner of New York's The Meatball Shop has a thing for caviar. On nachos. "I first made nachos with caviar and crème fraîche after an event that left me with a ton of trout roe," he explains. "I learned that tortilla chips are near perfect for caviar service, lending a crispy character seldom found in the more traditional blini, potatoes or seafood. I must admit, there was quite a bit of alcohol involved. Since then, I've paired caviar dip with tortilla chips at a few dinner parties. So it wasn't just the alcohol—this is actually a great combination."

✦ ✦

INGREDIENTS

Makes 4 servings

½ small red onion (or ¼ large), finely chopped

1 hardboiled egg

18 thin tortilla chips

1 cup crème fraîche or sour cream

4 ounces trout roe

2 ounces hackleback caviar (or your favorite caviar)

2 scallions, thinly sliced

DIRECTIONS

Soak the onion in water for 10 minutes, then drain and set aside.

Separate the egg yolk from the egg white. Pass each part through a fine-mesh sieve (use a rubber spatula to help press the egg through the sieve).

Arrange the chips in a single layer on a serving platter. Spoon a dollop of crème fraîche on top of each chip, followed by small spoonfuls of the trout roe and caviar. Sprinkle the onion, egg and scallions over the chips and serve immediately.

"THE FIRST TIME I MADE NACHOS WITH CAVIAR AND CRÈME FRAÎCHE,
THERE WAS QUITE A BIT OF ALCOHOL INVOLVED.
BUT I'VE TRIED IT SINCE—SOBER—AND IT'S ACTUALLY A GREAT COMBINATION."

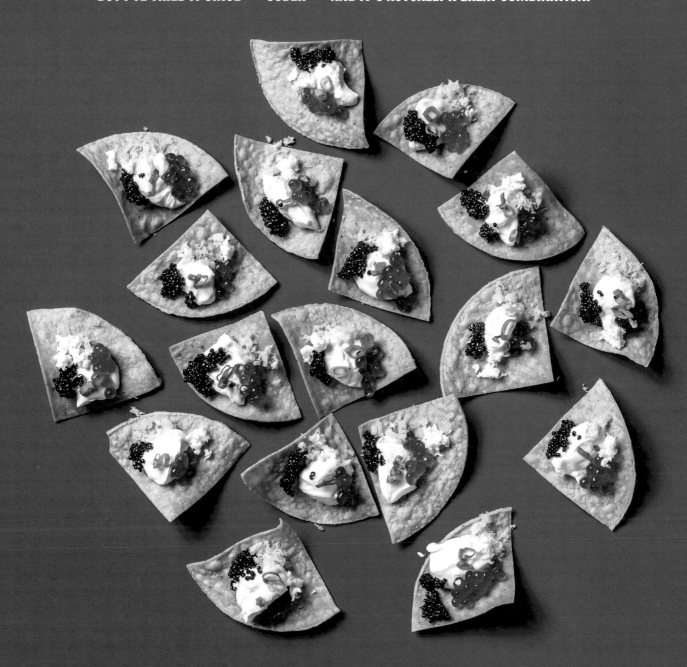

HEEBSTER NACHOS

GAIL SIMMONS

Top Chef judge, food critic and author Gail Simmons grew up in Toronto and Montreal, home to some of the world's best Jewish delis. She has since settled with her husband, Jeremy, and daughter, Dahlia, in Brooklyn, where she continues to schmear almost everything. That includes nachos. "These are totally silly and go against everything I hold dear about Mexican nachos," she says. "BUT. THEY ARE INSANELY DELICIOUS. And addictive. My friend Teresia and I made them and basically ate the whole platter standing up at my counter, leaving behind just three chips. Jeremy came home four hours later and devoured them, even though they were soggy and sad by then. That's when I knew I might be onto something."

✦ ✦

INGREDIENTS

Makes 4 to 6 servings

2 tablespoons sesame seeds

2 tablespoons poppy seeds

1 tablespoon dried shallots or onion powder

2 teaspoons garlic powder

1 teaspoon coarse salt

2 tablespoons canola oil

Six 8-inch whole wheat pitas

2 tablespoons capers—rinsed, drained and coarsely chopped

½ cup sour cream

8 ounces smoked whitefish, flaked into pieces, bones carefully removed

½ small red onion, thinly sliced

½ seedless English cucumber, peeled and diced

1 large tomato, diced

2 tablespoons chopped dill

DIRECTIONS

Place the oven rack in the middle position and preheat the oven to 350°.

In a small bowl, combine the sesame seeds, poppy seeds, shallots or onion powder, garlic powder and salt. You have just made your own Everything Bagel mix. Mazel tov!

Cut each pita into 8 even wedges. Tear or cut each wedge into 2 halves (each pita will yield 16 chips). Arrange the pita pieces in a single layer on a large baking sheet and brush with oil (use two baking sheets if necessary). Sprinkle each wedge liberally with Everything Bagel mix. Turn the wedges over and repeat the process with the oil and spice mix. Bake the pita until lightly golden and crisp, 7 to 10 minutes. Transfer the chips to a wire rack or plate and let cool.

Meanwhile, in a small bowl, fold the capers into the sour cream.

On a large platter, spread half the pita chips in a single layer, top with half of the sour cream mixture, whitefish, onion, cucumber and tomato. Repeat with the remaining chips, sour cream, fish and vegetables. Sprinkle with dill and serve immediately.

"THESE GO AGAINST EVERYTHING I HOLD DEAR ABOUT MEXICAN NACHOS. BUT. THEY ARE **INSANELY DELICIOUS.**"

DUCK CONFIT NACHOS

"Growing up in California, we had no shortage of chances to eat nachos," says Gabriel Rucker, the chef at Portland, Oregon's renowned Le Pigeon restaurant and author of *Le Pigeon: Cooking at the Dirty Bird*. It's safe to say he wasn't eating nachos like these during his childhood. Layered with duck confit, funky Taleggio cheese, tangy relish and honey, these babies have grown into fully functioning and sophisticated adults. "Side note," says Rucker, "these flavors also make great potato skins!"

INGREDIENTS

Makes 4 to 6 servings

3 duck confit legs (about 5 ounces each)

8 to 10 ounces tortilla chips (1 medium bag; Gabriel likes Juanitá's brand)

8 ounces Taleggio or other mild semisoft cheese, thinly sliced

1 cup Red Pepper Relish (page 142)

2 tablespoons buckwheat or other dark honey

½ cup sour cream

4 scallions, thinly sliced

2 jalapeños, thinly sliced (seeded, if desired)

½ cup chopped cilantro

Flaky sea salt

DIRECTIONS

Preheat the oven to 400°. Shred the meat from the duck confit legs and discard the bones and skin. Spread the chips out on a rimmed baking sheet and top with the shredded duck and cheese.

Bake until the cheese has melted, about 8 minutes. Top the nachos with about 1 cup of the relish and drizzle with the honey. Dollop the nachos with sour cream and scatter the scallions, jalapeños and cilantro over the top. Sprinkle with salt and serve.

"LAYERED WITH
DUCK CONFIT, FUNKY TALEGGIO, TANGY RELISH AND HONEY,
THESE ARE NOT THE NACHOS I GREW UP ON. THAT'S A GOOD THING."

BASTION NACHOS

Josh Habiger and Tom Bayless made a name for themselves at Nashville's much-lauded restaurant The Catbird Seat. When they opened their bar, Bastion, they wanted to serve one dish only: nachos. Why? "One reason: We really love nachos," say Habiger and Bayless. "Just like diner cheeseburgers, rectangle cafeteria pizza and gas station coffee, nachos are a nostalgic time jump. They can take you back to being a kid, sitting in the bleachers at a football game dipping mouth-woundingly salty corn chips into yellow cheese goop. Or crushing room-temperature Miller Lite at a college dive bar with those dudes you never saw again, eating Tostitos scattered with cubes of grill-marked chicken, powdery shredded cheddar cheese and one sliced black olive. Nachos are fun to eat, regardless of circumstance or quality. At Bastion, we tried to cover many of the nacho bases, taking attributes from the ballpark, the bar and the strip mall to create a new delicious memory."

INGREDIENTS

Makes 6 to 8 servings

12 to 16 ounces tortilla chips (1 large bag)

One 3- to 4-pound smoked or rotisserie chicken, shredded (about 2 cups of meat)

1 cup grated American cheese

1 cup Bastion Queso (page 132), warm

½ cup pickled jalapeño slices (from a jar or homemade; see page 142)

½ cup Pickled Red Onion (page 142)

½ cup sliced black olives

2 radishes, thinly sliced

½ cup chopped cilantro

½ cup sour cream

½ cup crumbled cotija cheese

1 cup Raw Tomatillo Salsa (page 133)

Black Hot Sauce (page 140), for serving

DIRECTIONS

Preheat the oven to 400°. Arrange half of the chips on a rimmed baking sheet. Scatter half of the chicken and American cheese over the chips. Repeat to form a second layer of chips, chicken and cheese. Bake until the cheese has melted, about 5 to 7 minutes.

Pour a generous amount of queso over the chips. Arrange the remaining toppings over the chips and serve with the tomatillo salsa and hot sauce on the side and/or drizzled over the nachos.

"NACHOS ARE A NOSTALGIC TIME JUMP. WE TOOK ATTRIBUTES FROM THE BALLPARK, THE BAR AND THE STRIP MALL TO CREATE

A NEW DELICIOUS MEMORY."

NACHOS WITH CHICKEN TINGA

The nachos at Brooklyn's River Styx restaurant have developed a following for their ooey-gooey cheese sauce. "It's the best stadium cheese imaginable," says chef Homer Murray, "as if Wrigley Field made you nachos for your birthday. Melt American cheese, cream, hot sauce and pickled jalapeños together until the mixture is the consistency you would want to rub on a loved one." Murray tops his chips with said cheese sauce, braised chicken and crema. Murray adds: "It is recommended to cruise from component to component separately until you're ultimately doing what everyone does, which is shove the whole bloody plate down your gullet with the palm of your hand."

✦ ✦

INGREDIENTS

Makes 4 to 6 servings

2 boneless, skinless chicken breasts

One 12-ounce bottle Negra Modelo beer

2 arbol chiles

Kosher salt

1 cup heavy cream

8 ounces American cheese (not processed), grated (2 cups)

¾ cup pickled jalapeños (from a jar or homemade; see page 142), ¼ cup finely chopped and ½ cup of slices

2 tablespoons hot sauce (Homer likes Crystal brand)

Kosher salt, to taste

½ cup sour cream

3 tablespoons mayonnaise

1 tablespoon fresh lime juice

8 to 10 ounces tortilla chips (1 medium bag)

5 radishes, thinly sliced

1 cup cilantro leaves

2 tablespoons finely chopped chives

DIRECTIONS

Cook the chicken: In a medium saucepan, combine the chicken, beer, chiles and 2 teaspoons of salt. Bring the mixture to a simmer over medium-high heat and continue to simmer until the chicken is cooked through, about 10 minutes. Remove the pan from the heat and let the chicken cool in the liquid before shredding into bite-size pieces.

Make the queso: In a small saucepan, combine the cream, cheese, chopped jalapeños and hot sauce. Cook over medium heat, stirring, until the cheese has melted and a thick sauce has formed, about 10 minutes. Season to taste with salt and keep warm.

Make the crema: In a small bowl, whisk together the sour cream, mayonnaise and lime juice. Season with salt and set aside.

Arrange the chips on a rimmed baking sheet. Top with the shredded chicken and pour the queso over the top. Drizzle the crema over the chips. Garnish with the radishes, pickled jalapeño slices, cilantro and chives. Serve.

"THESE NACHOS ARE MADE WITH THE **BEST STADIUM CHEESE IMAGINABLE,** AS IF

WRIGLEY FIELD MADE YOU NACHOS FOR YOUR BIRTHDAY."

CHICKEN GUMBO NACHOS

David Guas's restaurant Bayou Bakery might be located in Virginia, but the author of the dessert cookbook *Dam Good Sweet* is always thinking about his hometown of New Orleans. "I live to share the cuisine from my native foodways," he says. "So when the nacho craving hits, I gotta give it a little Cajun lovin' and smother it with all the elements of a gumbo I grew up making with my Aunt Boo. (One change: I've swapped out the roux for Creole Mornay sauce. We're talking nachos, after all.) And since it's the South, we've got to have pickled okra. Rule number 1: Don't forget the Holy Trinity (that would be onion, celery and bell pepper). Rule number 2: Share with friends."

✦ ✦

INGREDIENTS

Makes 6 to 8 servings

3 tablespoons canola oil

1 cup diced sweet onion

½ cup diced green bell peppers

½ cup diced celery

1 tablespoon finely chopped garlic

1 pound andouille sausage links, coarsely chopped

12 ounces tortilla chips (1 large bag)

2 cups shredded chicken (preferably dark meat)

1 cup Creole Queso (page 130)

1 cup pickled okra, cut crosswise into ¼-inch slices

4 scallions, thinly sliced

DIRECTIONS

In a medium skillet, heat the oil over medium-high heat. Add the onion and cook, stirring, for 1 minute. Add the bell pepper, celery and garlic and cook, stirring, until the vegetables have softened, about 5 minutes. Transfer to a bowl and set aside.

In a food processor, pulse the chopped sausage until evenly ground. Heat the skillet used for the vegetables over medium heat. Add the sausage and cook until browned and slightly crispy, 5 to 7 minutes. Transfer the sausage to a bowl and set aside.

Preheat the oven to 400°. Arrange half of the chips on a rimmed baking sheet. Scatter half of the sausage and half of the chicken over the chips. Using a spoon, drizzle half of the queso over the meat. Scatter half of the vegetables and okra over the cheese. Repeat to make a second layer. Bake until the cheese has melted and the edges of the chips begin to brown, about 10 minutes. Garnish with the scallions and serve.

"RULE NUMBER 1: DON'T FORGET THE HOLY TRINITY (THAT'D BE ONION, CELERY AND BELL PEPPER). **RULE NUMBER 2: SHARE WITH FRIENDS."**

BREAKFAST NACHOS

"Growing up in Southern California, nachos were something of a weekly craving," says Tiffani Thiessen. The actress who played Kelly Kapowski on *Saved by the Bell* and Valerie Malone on *Beverly Hills, 90210* is now a food and entertaining personality with a show (*Dinner at Tiffani's*) on the Cooking Channel. Here, she's reimagined her childhood craving into a breakfast-worthy dish that tends to disappear "within three to four minutes after serving."

INGREDIENTS

Makes 4 to 6 servings

12 ounces breakfast sausages, casings removed

1 yellow onion, diced

2 red bell peppers, seeded and diced

1 bunch kale, tough stems discarded and leaves cut into ½-inch ribbons

½ cup mayonnaise

6 tablespoons Sriracha hot sauce

Pinch of sugar

4 to 6 eggs

8 to 10 ounces large, sturdy potato chips

DIRECTIONS

Heat a large skillet over medium-high heat. Add the sausages and cook, breaking them up into chunks with a spoon as they cook, until browned and cooked through, about 10 minutes. Using a slotted spoon, transfer the cooked sausage to a bowl, leaving any fat in the pan.

Add the onion and peppers to the skillet and cook, stirring occasionally, until softened, about 5 minutes. Transfer the vegetables to the bowl with the sausage. Add the kale to the same skillet and cook until wilted, about 2 minutes. Turn off the heat.

In a small bowl, whisk together the mayonnaise, Sriracha and sugar.

In a large nonstick skillet, fry the eggs over medium-high heat to desired doneness.

Arrange the potato chips on a platter and top with the sausage, onion and peppers. Scatter the kale over the nachos, top with the fried eggs, drizzle with the Sriracha mayo and serve.

"GROWING UP IN SOUTHERN CALIFORNIA,

NACHOS WERE SOMETHING OF A
WEEKLY CRAVING."

DOROTHY'S POT-ROAST NACHOS

GAVIN KAYSEN

After a seven-year stint as executive chef at NYC's Café Boulud, Gavin Kaysen returned to his home state of Minnesota to open Spoon and Stable. The menu includes a version of his grandmother Dorothy's pot roast, now a perennial favorite. "My grandmother and I cooked and baked together when I was a kid, so it only seemed right to put her pot roast on my menu," Kaysen says. "When thinking about the perfect nacho, I decided to combine two of my favorites: her pot roast and cheese curds, a specialty to this part of the country." The result is a Midwestern take on the Canadian dish poutine, which combines French fries with cheese curds and gravy.

INGREDIENTS

Makes 4 to 6 servings

2 tablespoons canola oil

2 to 2½ pounds top blade beef

Salt and freshly ground black pepper

2 tablespoons unsalted butter

1 medium red onion, quartered

2 medium carrots, cut into 2-inch pieces

2 celery stalks, cut into 2-inch pieces

4 button or baby portobello mushrooms, halved

1 medium parsnip, cut into 2-inch pieces

4 garlic cloves, halved

½ cup tomato paste

1 bay leaf

1 rosemary sprig

1 cup dry red wine

2 cups beef broth

8 to 10 ounces tortilla chips (1 medium bag)

8 ounces fresh cheese curds

½ cup Harissa Aioli (page 141)

3 scallions, thinly sliced on the bias

½ cup coarsely chopped cilantro

DIRECTIONS

Preheat the oven to 350°. Heat the oil in a large saucepan or Dutch oven over high heat. Season the meat all over with salt and pepper. Sear the meat until deeply browned on all sides, about 2 minutes a side. Transfer the meat to a plate; add the butter, onion, carrots, celery, mushrooms, parsnip and garlic to the pan. Cook the vegetables, stirring frequently, until they begin to soften, about 5 minutes. Add the tomato paste and cook until you see the oil start to separate from the tomato. Add the herbs and wine, bring to a strong simmer and cook until the sauce begins to thicken, about 2 minutes. Return the beef to the pan, add the broth, cover and cook until the meat is very tender, about 3 hours.

Preheat the oven to 400°. Remove the meat from the pan and shred it into bite-size chunks. Save about ½ cup of braising liquid for finishing the nachos. (The leftover vegetables are also delicious and can be repurposed, or you can add the vegetables to the nachos as well, if desired.)

Arrange the chips on a rimmed baking sheet and top with some of the meat. Scatter the cheese curds over the top and bake until the cheese has melted slightly, 5 to 7 minutes. Drizzle the harissa aioli and some of the reserved braising liquid over the nachos, garnish with scallions and cilantro and serve.

"MY GRANDMOTHER'S POT ROAST PLUS CHEESE CURDS IS LIKE

POUTINE ON STEROIDS."

PERFECT BITE NACHOS

TIM HOLLINGSWORTH

Timothy Hollingsworth, the former chef de cuisine at the French Laundry who's now heading up L.A.'s Otium and Barrel & Ashes, might have a fancy cooking background, but he's no stranger to the nacho. "When I was younger, my grandpa would make nachos for us, and he always made sure that each chip was the perfect bite. He used to line up the chips on a plate, top each with a slice of Tillamook cheddar, a dash of picante salsa, an olive and a dollop of sour cream. Cooked in the microwave until everything was melted, these nachos were the perfect bite every time. Meanwhile, my dad would be grilling up Santa Maria–style tri tip, which would end up chopped up on top of our nachos—if we hadn't yet finished them."

INGREDIENTS

Makes 4 to 6 servings

½ cup olive oil

1 medium yellow onion, quartered

3 tablespoons chopped garlic

1 bunch thyme, chopped

¼ cup balsamic vinegar

1 tablespoon onion powder

1 tablespoon garlic powder

¼ teaspoon cayenne

¼ teaspoon red pepper flakes

1 beef tri-tip roast (about 2 pounds)

Salt and freshly ground black pepper

8 to 10 ounces tortilla chips
(1 medium bag)

8 ounces sliced cheddar cheese

8 ounces sliced Monterey Jack cheese

1 cup Classic Guacamole (page 139)

Sour cream

1 cup Pico de Gallo (page 137)

DIRECTIONS

Marinate the beef: In a large mixing bowl, combine the oil, onion, garlic, thyme, vinegar, onion powder, garlic powder, cayenne and red pepper flakes. Add the beef, cover and refrigerate for at least 6 hours (or up to overnight).

Prepare a two-stage grill with high and medium-low sides. Season the beef with salt and pepper, place on the hot side of the grill and sear, turning once, until charred on both sides, about 3 minutes a side. Move the meat to the medium-low side of the grill and continue grilling, turning the meat over every 10 minutes or so, until an instant-read thermometer inserted in the thickest part of the meat reaches 140° for medium, about 35 to 40 minutes total. Transfer the meat to a cutting board and let rest for 15 minutes before cutting into ½-inch dice. (You will have leftover beef; start by cutting about 2 cups' worth and reserve the rest for another use.)

Working in batches, arrange the chips on a microwave-safe plate. Top each chip with half a slice each of cheddar and Monterey Jack. Microwave the nachos at full power just until the cheese melts, about 30 to 45 seconds. Top each chip with a piece or two of beef, a dollop each of guacamole and sour cream and a spoonful of pico de gallo. Repeat with the remaining ingredients and serve.

"MY GRANDPA WOULD MAKE NACHOS FOR US, AND HE ALWAYS MADE SURE THAT EACH TORTILLA CHIP WAS

THE PERFECT BITE."

PINEAPPLE-BACON NACHOS

J. KENJI

"These nachos are the result of a late-night, stumbling raid to my fridge," says J. Kenji López-Alt, the managing culinary director of Serious Eats and author of *The Food Lab* cookbook. "There I found a stack of bacon, Brie cheese, a pineapple and leftover salsa. The combination may seem odd at first glance, but if you think about it, it's essentially the same flavors as tacos al pastor, with the ratio of pork to pineapple reversed. So instead of pineapple-seasoned pork, you have pork-seasoned pineapple. The Brie works really well: Its nuttiness reminds me of Swiss cheese on a good Cubano sandwich. You can make these in a big pile, but I prefer them as individually topped bites so that you have the perfect ratio on each chip."

INGREDIENTS

Makes 4 to 6 servings

½ pound slab bacon, cut into 2-by-1-by-½-inch slices

½ pound fresh pineapple, peel and core removed, cut into ½-inch dice (about 2 cups)

Kosher salt and freshly ground black pepper

2 chipotle chiles in adobo, plus 1 tablespoon adobo sauce

3 tablespoons freshly squeezed orange juice

8 to 10 ounces Homemade Tortilla Chips (page 124) or store-bought tortilla chips

8 ounces Brie cheese, sliced thinly

1 cup Charred Salsa Verde (page 136)

1 red jalapeño or Fresno chile, thinly sliced crosswise

Cilantro leaves, for garnish

DIRECTIONS

Cook the bacon pieces in a medium nonstick or cast-iron skillet over medium heat, turning frequently, until crisp. Transfer to a paper towel–lined plate and set aside. (Do not wipe out the skillet.) Add the pineapple to the hot bacon grease, toss to coat and cook, stirring occasionally, until tender and lightly browned, about 5 minutes. Season to taste with salt and pepper and transfer to a plate.

In a blender or the jar of an immersion blender, combine the chipotle chiles, adobo sauce and orange juice. Blend into a smooth puree. Season to taste with salt and pepper and set aside.

Place the oven rack in the middle position and preheat the oven to 425°. Spread a single layer of chips on a rimmed baking sheet. Top each chip with some pineapple, a piece or two of bacon and a thin slice of Brie. Bake until the Brie has melted and bubbly, about 2 minutes. Top each chip with a spoonful of charred salsa verde, a slice of chile and a little cilantro. Drizzle with the chipotle sauce and serve immediately.

"THIS IS THE RESULT OF A STUMBLING RAID TO MY FRIDGE LATE AT NIGHT —OFTEN THE BEST TIME FOR NACHOS."

WEEKEND NACHOS

Georgia restaurateur and *Top Chef* judge Hugh Acheson believes that the weekend is for letting creativity dictate nachos. "Start by making some beer-braised beef short ribs," Acheson says. "And fancy that, you made too many! With the leftovers, you will make nachos. In this idealized experience, you will frolic in the woods, foraging for ramps. You are dressed like a gnome, but nobody cares. You get back to the kitchen and have some pressure-cooked pintos all ready to go. Let's build some nachos: Take the beef plus pintos plus jack cheese, pickled peppers, those ramps all charred and tasty and assemble it all over tasty white corn tortilla chips, which maybe you made yourself. That gets baked until crisp and gooey and melty, and then you get all Jackson Pollock when the crema comes out. You eat and drink a beer, all the while wearing that gnome uniform with pride."

INGREDIENTS

Makes 4 to 6 servings

1 tablespoon vegetable oil, plus more for the ramps

2 pounds boneless chuck roast

Kosher salt and freshly ground black pepper

1 large onion, thinly sliced

4 cloves garlic, smashed

One 12-ounce bottle Negra Modelo beer

One 15-ounce can pinto beans, drained

1 bunch ramps (about 8 ramps) or scallions, root ends trimmed

8 to 10 ounces tortilla chips (1 medium bag)

8 ounces Monterey Jack cheese, grated (2 cups)

½ cup sliced pickled Fresno or jalapeño peppers

1 cup Homemade Crema (page 141) or sour cream

DIRECTIONS

Preheat the oven to 400°. Heat the oil in a large heavy-bottomed saucepan or Dutch oven over medium-high heat. Season the beef all over with salt and pepper and sear it on all sides until well browned, about 3 minutes a side. Transfer the meat to a plate. Add the onion and garlic to the pan and cook over medium-low heat, stirring occasionally, until the onion has caramelized and is very soft, about 20 minutes. Add the beer and, using a wooden spoon, scrape up any browned bits on the bottom of the pan. Return the beef to the pan, cover and roast, checking every 30 minutes, until the beef shreds easily with a fork, 2 to 3 hours. When the meat is cool enough to handle, shred it into its braising liquid, then stir in the beans.

Meanwhile, preheat the broiler. Place the ramps on a rimmed baking sheet, brush with oil and season with salt. Broil the ramps, turning every 30 seconds or so, until charred all over, 2 to 3 minutes total. Transfer to a cutting board and chop coarsely.

Scatter half of the chips on a rimmed baking sheet. Scatter half of the cheese over the chips. Repeat to make a second layer. Broil the chips until the cheese has melted, about 2 minutes. Top the chips with the shredded beef–bean mixture and broil again to heat the meat through, about 1 minute. Top with the charred ramps and pickled peppers. Drizzle the crema over the top and serve.

"YOU HAVE FROLICKED IN THE WOODS...

DRESSED LIKE A GNOME.

YOU HAVE SOME PRESSURE-COOKED PINTOS, ALL READY TO GO. YOU GET ALL

JACKSON POLLOCK WHEN THE CREMA COMES OUT."

NACHOS IN A BAG

KRISTEN KISH

"I am a traditionalist when it comes to nachos, and my gold star goes to the 'walking taco,'" says Kristen Kish, winner of *Top Chef* Season 10. "I'm talking about the old-school, cafeteria hot lunch–style walking taco. Individual bags of chips filled with grated cheddar cheese, taco meat, sour cream, chopped onion, pickled jalapeño, canned black olives, tomatoes and whatever else you could find at the salad bar. I was known to top it all off with a little ranch dressing and buttery corn. You roll the top of the paper bag closed, shake it, then dig in with a plastic spork. The chips are evenly coated, every bite drenched, your knuckles kissed by the flavors as you dig for that last bite in the bottom corner. When I was a kid, it was fun. As an adult, it's fuel for nights of too many drinks and filthy one-night stands. And a plastic spork will make it taste better, I promise."

✦ ✦

INGREDIENTS

Makes 4 servings

1 pound ground beef

1 teaspoon salt

1 teaspoon chile powder

1 teaspoon cumin

½ teaspoon freshly ground black pepper

½ teaspoon smoked paprika

¼ teaspoon cayenne pepper

¼ teaspoon coriander

¼ cup tomato paste

½ cup water

Juice of 1 lime

8 to 10 ounces tortilla chips (1 medium bag)

1 cup grated sharp cheddar cheese

¼ cup chopped red onion

¼ cup pickled jalapeño slices (from a jar or homemade; see page 142)

½ cup cooked corn kernels

½ cup sliced black olives

1 large tomato, cored and diced

½ cup sour cream

¼ cup bottled ranch dressing

DIRECTIONS

Heat a large skillet over medium-high heat. Add the beef and cook, stirring and breaking the meat up with a spoon, until well browned, 8 to 10 minutes. Stir in the spices and tomato paste and cook, stirring, for 1 minute. Add the water, bring to a simmer and cook until the meat has absorbed the liquid, about 5 minutes. Turn off the heat and stir in the lime juice. Set aside.

Divide the chips among 4 brown-paper lunch bags or small chip bags. (You can also serve the nachos in 4 bowls.) Divide the meat, cheese, onion, jalapeño slices, corn, olives, tomato, sour cream and ranch dressing among the bags. Close and shake the bags well to distribute the ingredients. Serve with forks.

"THE CHIPS ARE EVENLY COATED, **EVERY BITE DRENCHED**, YOUR KNUCKLES KISSED BY THE FLAVORS AS YOU DIG FOR THAT LAST BITE

IN THE BOTTOM CORNER."

SMOKED MEAT POUTINE NACHOS

"Whether Canadians like it or not, Americans think of poutine as the food of Canada," says Noah Bernamoff, the founder of Mile End, NYC's fantastic Montreal-style deli. "To Canadians, it's just a snack." Albeit, he admits, an important one. "It's consumed when you're less than sober—or when you're just off the hockey rink and looking for something warm, greasy and filling." The dish, of course, is on the menu at Mile End, where they've swapped out fries for tortilla chips on Cinco de Mayo. "Fries are fried and salty; chips are fried and salty," says Bernamoff. "It just works."

✦ ✦

INGREDIENTS

Makes 4 to 6 servings

1 pound Montreal-style smoked meat or pastrami, unsliced

4 cups chicken broth, divided

¾ cup poutine gravy mix (Noah likes Berthelet brand)

8 to 10 ounces tortilla chips (1 medium bag)

½ pound fresh cheese curds, larger curds broken up

1 small red onion, diced

½ cup pickled jalapeño slices (from a jar or homemade; see page 142)

½ cup chopped cilantro

DIRECTIONS

Add an inch of water to a medium saucepan and place a steam insert inside the pan. Bring the water to a simmer and place the meat in the steamer. Cover the pot and steam the meat until it's very tender, about 1 hour. Turn off the heat and leave the pot covered to keep the meat warm.

Place 1 cup of broth in a bowl and whisk in the gravy mix until smooth. In a medium saucepan, bring the remaining 3 cups of broth to a boil. Add the cold stock–gravy mixture to the hot broth, whisking until the liquid becomes smooth and velvety. Keep the gravy warm over low heat, whisking occasionally.

Meanwhile, preheat the oven to 450°. Arrange half of the chips in a single layer on a rimmed baking sheet. Scatter half of the cheese curds over the top. Repeat to make a second layer of chips and cheese. Bake until the cheese curds have melted slightly, about 6 to 8 minutes.

While the chips bake, transfer the meat to a cutting board and pull it apart into bite-size pieces. Scatter the meat over the chips. Sprinkle the onion and jalapenos over the top and ladle a generous amount of gravy over the nachos. Sprinkle with cilantro and serve.

"POUTINE IS **CANADA'S GO-TO SNACK,** AND SUBBING OUT FRIES FOR TORTILLA CHIPS JUST WORKS."

BEST NACHOS OF ALL TIME

When Andrew Zimmern isn't circling the globe for his hit TV show *Bizarre Foods*, he's home cooking for his wife and 11-year-old son, Noah. "I serve this dish all the time at house parties, both for adults and for kids," Zimmern says. "My son grew up eating spicy foods: Kids are more adventurous than we give them credit for. These super-sophisticated nachos are built with several components, all made from scratch and delicious on their own. When served together, they will blow your mind. I wouldn't ask you to go through all of this work if you couldn't use these elements in other dishes: The queso fundido makes a great dip; the seven-pepper salsa is a great rub for steaks, pork or chicken; the tomatillo-and-avocado salsa is superb spooned over grilled fish, shrimp or lobster. You get the drift."

INGREDIENTS

Makes 4 to 6 servings

1 pound fresh Mexican chorizo, casings removed

1 large yellow onion, finely chopped

2 cups Seven-Pepper Salsa (page 137)

8 ounces queso Oaxaca or fresh mozzarella, grated (2 cups)

8 ounces grated Monterey Jack cheese (2 cups)

8 to 10 ounces tortilla chips (1 medium bag)

1 cup Avocado-Tomatillo Salsa (page 138)

½ cup cilantro leaves

1 cup diced fresh tomatoes

½ cup finely chopped red onion

1 cup sliced canned black olives

½ cup grated cotija cheese

2 limes, quartered, for serving

DIRECTIONS

Make the queso fundido: Preheat a large skillet over medium-high heat. Crumble the chorizo into the skillet and cook, breaking the meat up with a spoon, until the meat is browned, 5 to 7 minutes. Add the onion and cook until softened, about 4 minutes. Add the salsa, lower the heat to medium and bring the mixture to a simmer. Cook until any liquid evaporates, 5 to 7 minutes. Add the cheeses and stir for 1 minute. Turn off the heat and continue stirring until all of the cheese has melted.

Scatter the chips on a serving platter. Ladle about half of the queso fundido over the chips. Spoon a cup or more of the avocado-tomatillo salsa around the pile wherever the queso didn't land.

Sprinkle with the cilantro, tomatoes, onion and olives. Sprinkle the cotija cheese over the top. Serve with lime wedges.

"I WOULDN'T ASK YOU TO GO THROUGH ALL OF THIS WORK IF **YOU COULDN'T USE THESE ELEMENTS IN OTHER DISHES.**"

CHEESEBURGER NACHOS

PATRICK BERTOLETTI

At his Chicago restaurant, Taco in A Bag, the competitive eater Patrick "Deep Dish" Bertoletti serves a dozen varieties of portable nachos. This cheeseburger version is the most popular, both with regulars and critics. (*Time Out Chicago* named it number 15 on its list of "100 Best Things to Eat in 2015.") The secret, Bertoletti says, is to "hit everything in your mouth all at once." There's richness from the meat, cheese and mayo; crunch from the chips and potato straws; tartness from the banana peppers; sweetness from the barbecue sauce and brown sugar; and savoriness from the seasoned salt. "All my layers of flavors stand alone. When you put it all together, there's no way it could be bad," says Bertoletti.

✦ ✦

INGREDIENTS

Makes 4 to 6 servings

1 tablespoon vegetable oil

1 pound ground beef

Kosher salt

Lawry's Seasoned Salt

½ cup mayonnaise

¼ cup ketchup

2 tablespoons barbecue sauce (Patrick likes Sweet Baby Ray's brand)

2 tablespoons dark brown sugar

8 to 10 ounces tortilla chips (1 medium bag)

1 cup Four-Cheese Queso (page 132), warmed

2 cups shredded romaine lettuce

1 cup diced tomatoes

1 cup diced banana peppers

2 cups prepared shoestring potatoes (such as Pik-Nik brand)

DIRECTIONS

Heat the oil in large skillet over medium-high heat. Add the beef, a large pinch each of salt and seasoned salt, and cook the meat until well browned and cooked through, about 4 minutes. Season to taste with more salt and/or seasoned salt; set aside and keep warm.

Make the special sauce: In a mixing bowl, whisk together the mayonnaise, ketchup, barbecue sauce and sugar. Season to taste with salt and set aside.

Arrange the chips on serving platter and top with the meat. Drizzle the cheese sauce over the meat. Scatter the lettuce, tomatoes, peppers and potato straws over the top, drizzle with special sauce and serve.

"ALL MY LAYERS OF FLAVORS STAND ALONE. WHEN YOU PUT IT ALL TOGETHER, **THERE'S NO WAY IT COULD BE BAD.**"

NUEVO SUD NACHOS

JOHN T. EDGE

John T. Edge is a renowned food writer and director of the Southern Foodways Alliance, so he knows from Southern food. Here, he interprets nachos in Southern style with pickled okra and pulled pork. "I smoke a lot of pork butt in my backyard," he says. And what better way to use it? The guacamole comes from his wife, Blair, who blends yogurt into her recipe, "not because it's healthy, but because it tastes great," says Edge.

INGREDIENTS

Makes 4 to 6 servings

2 ripe avocados—halved, pitted and diced

1½ cups plain yogurt

1 bunch cilantro, bottom halves of stems discarded, plus ½ cup chopped cilantro, divided

Juice of 1 lime, plus more to taste

Pinch of cumin (optional)

Hot sauce, to taste (optional)

Salt and freshly ground black pepper

8 to 10 ounces tortilla chips (1 medium bag)

2 cups leftover pulled pork

1 cup cheddar cheese

1 cup prepared salsa verde (John T. likes Herdez brand)

½ cup chopped white onion

½ cup chopped pickled okra

½ cup chopped cilantro

DIRECTIONS

In a food processor, combine the avocado, yogurt, bunch of cilantro, lime juice, cumin (if using) and hot sauce (if using). Process until smooth and season to taste with salt, pepper and more lime juice, if needed. Transfer to a bowl, cover with plastic wrap and refrigerate until ready to use.

Preheat the oven to 450°. Arrange the chips on a rimmed baking sheet. Scatter the pork over the chips and top with the cheddar. Bake the chips until the cheese has melted and the edges of the chips begin to brown, about 8 minutes. Spoon the yogurt guacamole and salsa verde over the chips, sprinkle with the onion, okra and cilantro and serve.

"I SMOKE A LOT OF PORK BUTT

IN MY BACKYARD, AND WE OFTEN MAKE NACHOS

FROM LEFTOVER BUTT, SALSA VERDE, CHEDDAR
AND CHOPPED PICKLED OKRA."

ANTIPASTO NACHOS

ZAHRA TANGORRA

At her dearly departed Brooklyn neighborhood restaurant Brucie, Zahra Tangorra would create a new version of nachos almost every night. "It's a hard thing to serve nachos at an Italian comfort-food restaurant, but we figured out how to do it," Tangorra says. She started by focusing on Italian flavors, but eventually said, "Screw it: We're going to make any nachos we want and people will love them." Why nachos? "They are absolutely my favorite food, for starters," she says. "They are the perfect vessel for the right mix of textures and temperatures, creaminess and fattiness and spiciness." These antipasto-inspired nachos were Tangorra's favorite: "Italian-American food is my heart. It's everything I crave, love and admire about food. So to translate all that to a nacho was perfect."

✦ ✦

INGREDIENTS

Makes 4 to 6 servings

1 cup diced soppressata (or your favorite Italian cured sausage)

8 to 10 ounces tortilla chips (preferably homemade; see page 124, or 1 medium bag)

1 cup Provolone Queso (page 131), warmed

½ cup diced pepperoncini

½ cup diced roasted red peppers

⅓ cup diced marinated artichoke hearts

⅓ cup sliced black olives

⅓ cup diced red onions

1 cup shredded iceberg lettuce

¼ cup chopped parsley

⅓ cup Spicy Pizza Shop Vinaigrette (page 140)

Parmigiano-Reggiano cheese, for shaving

DIRECTIONS

Place the soppressata in a medium skillet and set over medium-high heat. Cook the soppressata, stirring occasionally, until crisp and browned all over, about 4 minutes.

Arrange the chips on a serving platter and drizzle some of the queso over the top. Add the remaining toppings and drizzle the vinaigrette over the nachos. Using a vegetable peeler, shave some Parmesan on top of the nachos and serve.

"NACHOS ARE THE PERFECT VESSEL FOR THE RIGHT MIX OF TEXTURES AND TEMPERATURES,

CREAMINESS AND **FATTINESS** AND **SPICINESS.**"

BAR NACHOS

Jon Shook and Vinny Dotolo are the reigning kings of the Los Angeles dining scene, having launched a growing family of always-packed restaurants, which include Animal and Son of a Gun. Trois Familia, a French-Mexican brunch spot, is their third collaboration with the French chef Ludo Lefebvre. The initial menu included "French Nachos," with Mornay sauce, broccoli-jalapeño and chipotle-squash salsas. "We really liked that version," they said, and such critics as Jonathan Gold agreed, "but guests were split on them." They replaced the dish with a more traditional American bar nacho, which diners loved. Although they no longer serve these nachos at their restaurant, they often make them at home. "We decided that nachos are better with a beer while watching a game than for brunch." Of course, there's no rule against making these in the morning and serving them with beer.

✦ ✦

INGREDIENTS

Makes 4 to 6 servings

1 tablespoon canola oil

1 pound ground beef

1 tablespoon taco or chili spice blend (your favorite brand)

Kosher salt

½ cup water

8 to 10 ounces tortilla chips (1 medium bag)

1 cup Refried Black Beans (page 133)

1 cup Animal Queso (page 131)

½ cup pickled jalapeño slices (from a jar or homemade; see page 142)

2 tablespoons crème fraîche

2 cups shredded iceberg or romaine lettuce

DIRECTIONS

Heat the oil in a large skillet over high heat. Add the beef and cook, breaking it up with a spoon, until browned all over, about 3 minutes. Drain the fat from the pan and return it to the heat. Stir in the spice blend, salt and water. Bring to a simmer and cook the meat until the liquid evaporates, 3 to 5 minutes. Season to taste with salt.

Scatter the chips on a serving platter. Spread the refried beans on top, followed by the meat. Drizzle some of the queso over the meat. Scatter the jalapeños over the top, add the crème fraîche, sprinkle the lettuce on top and serve.

"WE RECOMMEND SERVING THESE NACHOS WITH
BEER, DURING A GAME."

MORCILLA NACHOS

Before opening their massive, hugely successful restaurant Toro in New York City, chefs Jamie Bissonnette and Ken Oringer took a scouting trip to Spain. At Tapas 24 in Barcelona, they were blown away by the "morcilla brava bomb," a large potato-and-blood-sausage croquette topped with aioli. "We loved it because it had so many textures and flavors," they said. "We couldn't stop eating the brava bomb, and when we made these nachos with many of the same ingredients, it was the same!"

✦ ✦

INGREDIENTS

Makes 8 to 10 servings

3 tablespoons canola oil

2 garlic cloves, chopped

1 medium yellow onion, diced

Kosher salt

1½ teaspoons Urfa or ancho chile powder

1 pound morcilla (Spanish blood sausage), casings removed

1 cup canned tomato puree

16 to 20 ounces tortilla chips (2 medium bags)

½ cup Pickled Red Onion (page 142)

½ cup pickled jalapeño slices (from a jar or homemade; see page 142)

1 cup Idiazabal Queso (page 130), warm

6 ounces Tetilla cheese, grated (1½ cups)

3 large eggs

1 tablespoon olive oil

¼ cup chopped Manzanilla olives

2 tablespoons fried garlic (available at Asian markets)

½ cup thinly sliced scallions

½ cup Romesco Sauce (page 139)

DIRECTIONS

In a medium skillet, heat the canola oil over medium heat. Add the garlic and onion, sprinkle with salt and cook, stirring, until softened, about 4 minutes. Add the chile powder and morcilla, breaking the sausage up into small pieces with a spoon. Cook for 5 minutes, then add the tomato puree. Bring to a simmer and cook until thickened, about 10 minutes.

Preheat the oven to 350°. Arrange a third of the chips on a rimmed baking sheet. Top with dollops of the meat mixture and scatter a third of the pickled onions and jalapeños over the top. Drizzle some of the warm queso over the top. Repeat to make two more layers, scattering the Tetilla over the top layer. Bake the chips until the cheese has melted, about 8 to 10 minutes.

While the nachos bake, fry the eggs, sunny-side up, in the olive oil. Place the eggs on top of the nachos and scatter with the olives, garlic and scallions. Spoon some of the *romesco* over the nachos and serve.

"WE COULDN'T STOP EATING THE **BRAVA BOMB,** AND WHEN WE MADE THESE NACHOS, IT WAS THE SAME!"

LOTUS ROOT NACHOS
WITH BACON, KIMCHI & CREAMY CORN

HOONI KIM

"This appears to be a normal plate of Tex-Mex nachos until you look closer," says chef Hooni Kim, of NYC's modern-Korean restaurant Danji. "Then you realize the chips have holes in them, the red chili is made of kimchi, and instead of cheese, there's the corn *banchan* you see at Korean barbecue restaurants." The creamy corn, spicy mayo and sour cream replace the melted cheese ("Koreans don't do cheese"), and the kimchi, both cooked and fresh, cut that richness with a ton of fermented flavor. Kim has one suggestion: "Beer pairs well, but what's even better is an icy mug of *makgeolli* (Korean unfiltered rice beer)."

✦ ✦

INGREDIENTS

Makes 4 to 6 servings

For the lotus root chips:

2 medium to large lotus roots (about 1 pound total)

1 quart canola oil

1 tablespoon kosher salt

2 tablespoons *gochugaru* (Korean red pepper flakes)

For the spicy mayo:

3 tablespoons mayonnaise (preferably Kewpie brand)

2 tablespoons Sriracha hot sauce

For the creamy corn banchan:

1 ear of corn

1 tablespoon unsalted butter

Pinch of salt

2 tablespoons mayonnaise

For the BKO (bacon, kimchi and onion):

¼ pound slab bacon, diced

½ medium yellow onion, diced

1 cup finely chopped kimchi

Garnishes:

½ red onion, cut into ¼-inch dice

½ cup kimchi, cut into ¼-inch dice

2 tablespoons sour cream

3 scallions, thinly sliced

Hot sauce, for serving

DIRECTIONS

Make the lotus root chips: Peel the lotus roots and slice them crosswise into ⅛-inch rounds (use a mandoline if you have one). Place the lotus root slices in a bowl and run under cold water for 5 minutes to rinse away most of the starch.

In a medium saucepan, heat the oil until it reaches 325° on a deep-fry thermometer. Line a baking sheet with paper towels. In a small bowl, combine the salt and *gochugaru*.

Drain the lotus root slices and pat them very dry with paper towels. Working in small batches, fry the lotus root until golden brown, 3 to 4 minutes. Transfer the chips to the baking sheet and sprinkle with the salt-*gochugaru* mixture. Repeat with the remaining lotus root.

Make the spicy mayo: In a bowl, stir together the mayonnaise and Sriracha.

Make the creamy corn *banchan*: Cut the corn kernels from the cob. In a medium skillet, melt the butter over medium heat. Add the corn, season with salt and cook until tender, about 3 minutes. Transfer the corn to a bowl, stir in the mayonnaise and set aside.

Make the BKO: In a medium skillet, cook the bacon over medium heat until most of the fat has rendered and the bacon is browned and crispy, about 5 minutes. Add the onion and cook, stirring, until softened, about 4 minutes. Add the kimchi and cook until softened, about 5 minutes longer. Turn off the heat and set aside.

Assemble the chips: Arrange the lotus root chips on a platter. Spoon the spicy mayo over the chips. Scatter the red onion and corn *banchan* over the chips. Mound the BKO in the center of the chips; place a mound of the diced kimchi on one side and a mound of sour cream on the other. Sprinkle the scallions over the chips and serve with hot sauce.

"THIS APPEARS TO BE A **NORMAL PLATE OF TEX-MEX NACHOS**

UNTIL YOU LOOK CLOSER."

BRISKET NACHOS

DAN KLUGER

While he was cooking at Manhattan's ABC Kitchen, Dan Kluger racked up all kinds of awards (James Beard, *Food & Wine* "Best New Chef," etc.). The chef is known for cooking sophisticated dishes with hyper-local ingredients, but when times are tough, his ethos skews more downmarket. "I created this recipe when my family and I were between homes, and our living situation was rather uncomfortable and stressful (to say the least). We were staying at a friend's house that was on the market. Pretty much the only thing in this empty house was a working kitchen. I found myself constantly making my childhood comfort foods, which made the situation more bearable. One day I was craving nachos. As I started to assemble my ingredients, I realized I had leftover barbecue brisket that my friend Will had made. He's an avid pitmaster, and his brisket is one of the best I've ever had. Meaty, smoky and rich, it was the perfect addition to nachos."

INGREDIENTS

Makes 4 to 6 servings

8 to 10 ounces whole-grain tortilla chips

1½ cups peach salsa (Dan likes D.L. Jardine's brand)

1 cup canned black beans, drained

4 ounces sharp cheddar cheese, grated (1 cup)

4 ounces queso blanco or mozzarella cheese, grated (1 cup)

8 ounces barbecue brisket, cut into 1-inch pieces (about ⅛ inch thick)

1 to 2 jalapeño peppers, thinly sliced (seeded if desired)

½ cup coarsely chopped cilantro

¼ cup coarsely chopped mint leaves

½ cup plain Greek yogurt

Lime wedges, for serving

DIRECTIONS

Preheat the oven to 400°. Arrange a single layer of chips on a rimmed baking sheet. Drizzle the salsa over the chips, covering as many chips as possible. Top with two-thirds of the cheeses and the black beans.

Bake the nachos until the cheese has begun to melt, about 8 minutes. Remove from the oven and preheat the broiler. Top the chips with the brisket and remaining cheese and broil until the brisket is warmed through and the cheese is bubbling and begins to brown, 2 to 3 minutes. Top with the jalapeños, herbs and a few dollops of yogurt. Serve with lime wedges.

"MEATY, SMOKY AND RICH,

BRISKET IS THE PERFECT ADDITION TO NACHOS."

HI-LO NACHOS

"If you're making nachos and use Cool Ranch Doritos as your chip and Velveeta as your cheese, there is a 100 percent chance they will be the best thing you've ever eaten," says food writer Alison Roman, a veteran of *Bon Appétit* magazine. "Add a few fancier ingredients like fresh chorizo, watermelon radishes and Aleppo pepper, and it transcends deliciousness and becomes something truly magical. Kind of like wearing a Christian Lacroix sweater with a pair of $50 jeans. I'm pretty sure Anna Wintour doesn't eat nachos, but I'd like to think that if she did, she'd eat these."

INGREDIENTS

Makes 4 to 6 servings

1 pound fresh chorizo, removed from casings

1 large bag Cool Ranch Doritos

10 ounces Velveeta cheese, thinly sliced

2 watermelon radishes, thinly sliced

½ small red onion, thinly sliced

1 tablespoon fresh lime juice

1 teaspoon Aleppo pepper (or red pepper flakes)

Kosher salt

4 scallions, thinly sliced

1 cup chopped cilantro

¾ cup sour cream

Flaky sea salt

DIRECTIONS

Preheat the oven to 350°. In a large skillet, cook the chorizo over medium-high heat until it's cooked through and well browned, about 8 minutes. Remove from the heat.

Scatter a third of the chips over the bottom of a large cast-iron skillet. Top with a third of the chorizo and a third of the cheese. Repeat with the remaining chips, cheese and chorizo to make two more layers. Drizzle any leftover chorizo fat over the chips. Bake the chips until the cheese has melted and the chips are toasted, about 20 minutes.

Meanwhile, in a small bowl, toss the radishes, onion, lime juice and Aleppo pepper. Season to taste with salt and let the mixture sit, tossing occasionally.

When the nachos come out of the oven, top them with the radish-onion mixture, scallions and cilantro. Spoon the sour cream over the top, sprinkle with the flaky salt and serve.

"I'M PRETTY SURE **ANNA WINTOUR** DOESN'T EAT NACHOS,
BUT I'D LIKE TO THINK THAT IF SHE DID, SHE'D EAT THESE."

MERGUEZ NACHOS
WITH HARISSA & TEHINA

Michael Solomonov, the chef-owner of Philadelphia's Zahav restaurant, is perhaps America's premier Israeli food chef. He organizes annual trips to Israel with chefs from around the United States, and it was on one of those trips that he found inspiration for these pita nachos. "Imagine you're in Israel, waiting in line at a kebab shop at 2 a.m., salivating over the marinated meat dripping onto the hot coals in front of you. You're very hungry. At this exact moment, they take leftover pieces of pita, deep-fry them, toss them with za'atar and pass out cups of this snack to everyone in line." These nachos have become a staple in Solomonov's (admittedly extensive) snack food diet.

✦ ✦ ✦ ✦ ✦ ✦ ✦ ✦ ✦ ✦ ✦ ✦ ✦ ✦ ✦ ✦ ✦ ✦ ✦ ✦

INGREDIENTS

Makes 4 to 6 servings

Six 8-inch pitas

Olive oil

½ cup za'atar (available at Middle-Eastern markets)

2 garlic cloves, unpeeled

3 tablespoons fresh lemon juice

Kosher salt

½ cup tehina (tahini), stirred well

¼ teaspoon ground cumin

¼ to ½ cup ice water

1 pound merguez sausage, casings removed and sausage crumbled

½ cup harissa paste

½ cup black olives, pitted and chopped

1 cup cilantro leaves

DIRECTIONS

Make the pita chips: Preheat the oven to 350°. Cut each pita into 8 even wedges. Tear or cut each wedge into 2 halves (each pita will yield 16 chips). Arrange the pita pieces in a single layer on a large baking sheet and brush with oil (use two baking sheets if necessary). Bake for 15 minutes or until the chips are golden brown and crispy. Transfer the chips to paper towels and blot dry. Sprinkle with za'atar and set aside.

Make the tehina sauce: In a blender, combine the garlic, lemon juice and ¼ teaspoon of salt. Blend at high speed until the mixture forms a coarse puree. Let the mixture stand for 10 minutes to let the garlic flavor mellow. Pass the mixture through a fine-mesh strainer set over a large bowl, pressing on the solids to extract as much liquid as possible. Discard the solids. To the same bowl, add the tehina, cumin and ½ teaspoon of salt. Whisk the mixture until smooth, adding the ice water, about 3 tablespoons at a time, to thin out the mixture. The sauce will lighten in color as you whisk; if it seizes up, add more ice water, a bit at a time, whisking energetically, until you have a smooth, creamy sauce. Season to taste with more salt and cumin, if needed.

In a medium skillet, heat 1 tablespoon of oil over medium-high heat. Add the sausage and cook, stirring and breaking it up with a spoon, until well browned, 3 to 5 minutes. Turn off the heat.

Arrange a third of the pita chips on a serving platter. Drizzle a third of the tehina sauce over the chips. Spoon a third of the merguez and pan drippings over top of the tehina. Drizzle a third of the harissa over the top of the sausage. Sprinkle a third each of the olives and cilantro over the nachos. Repeat to make two more layers and serve.

"IN ISRAELI KEBAB SHOPS, THEY TAKE LEFTOVER PIECES OF PITA, DEEP-FRY THEM, TOSS THEM WITH ZA'ATAR AND PASS OUT CUPS OF THIS SNACK TO EVERYONE IN LINE."

HOT-COLD NACHO WREATH
WITH CHORIZO CREAM CHEESE

Ashley Christensen—whose restaurant group has transformed Raleigh, North Carolina, into a food destination—has turned any number of delicious leftovers, such as smoked pork or baked beans, into nachos. But this rendition, which employs a crazy-addictive chorizo–cream cheese dip, is her favorite. "I construct the nachos in a wreath formation so that the sour cream and tomato relish are in the middle for the cool-side-cool, hot-side-hot McDLT effect," she says, referencing the iconic 1980s McDonald's burger that separated the cold ingredients from the hot in the cardboard container. "One of the key ingredients to great nachos," says Christensen, "is the structural engineering of the dish."

✦ ✦

INGREDIENTS

Makes 4 to 6 servings

1 large tomato, diced

2 scallions, thinly sliced

Juice of half a lime

Salt

1 tablespoon vegetable oil

2 links (8 ounces) fresh chorizo sausage, casings removed

2 poblano chiles

One 8-ounce package cream cheese

8 to 10 ounces tortilla chips (1 medium bag)

2 cups mixed shredded cheese ("Mexican blend" or a mix of cheddar, Colby and Monterey Jack)

Sour cream

1 cup shredded romaine lettuce

DIRECTIONS

Preheat the oven to 400°. In a small bowl, toss the tomato and scallions with the lime juice and season to taste with salt.

In a skillet, heat the oil over medium-high heat. Add the chorizo and cook, breaking it up into small pieces with a spatula, until well browned, 5 to 7 minutes. Transfer the sausage to a bowl and set aside.

Roast the poblanos directly over the flame on a gas stove, turning frequently with tongs or a long-handled fork, until blackened all over, about 5 minutes. (Alternatively, broil the peppers about 2 inches from the heat source, turning frequently, until blackened all over, about 10 minutes.) Transfer the poblanos to a bowl and cover with plastic wrap; let stand until they're cool enough to handle. Rub the peppers with a paper towel to remove the skin. Cut off the tops of the peppers, then halve them. Discard the seeds and cut the peppers into ¼-inch dice. Add them to the bowl with the chorizo. Add the cream cheese and stir until mixed.

Arrange a layer of chips in a circular pattern on the baking sheet so it resembles a wreath. Sprinkle a third of the shredded cheese over the chips. Repeat to create two more layers of chips and cheese. Spoon the chorizo–cream cheese over the top of the chips. Bake until the cheese is melted and bubbling and the edges of the chips are starting to brown, 8 to 10 minutes.

Remove the nachos from the oven and slide them onto a serving platter, if desired. Mound the sour cream in the center of the circle and top with the tomato-scallion mixture. Sprinkle the lettuce over the nachos and serve.

"ONE OF THE KEY INGREDIENTS TO GREAT NACHOS IS THE
STRUCTURAL ENGINEERING
OF THE DISH."

GOCHUJANG CHILI-CHEESE NACHOS

Edward Lee—the Korean-American chef of Louisville's 610 Magnolia and MilkWood and author of the cookbook *Smoke and Pickles*—has long known what the rest of the country is just learning: Sweet-spicy-funky *gochujang* makes just about everything better. Here, he uses the Korean pantry staple in his beer-braised, chipotle-spiced beef chili and also mixes it into sour cream for extra umami and flavor. To make the nachos, he drapes the chile and creamy dip over tortilla chips, then adds crumbled cotija cheese and slices of fresh serrano peppers. "I eat nachos only a few times a year, so when I do, I want to make sure it's worth it," says Lee. "This recipe is not for the timid. It requires a long night, beers, whiskey and loud music."

✦ ✦

INGREDIENTS

Makes 4 to 6 servings

3 tablespoons vegetable oil, divided

2 pounds beef chuck roast, cut into ½-inch cubes

Salt and freshly ground black pepper

1 small onion, fine chopped

3 garlic cloves, finely chopped

1 jalapeño pepper, finely chopped

6 tablespoons plus 2 teaspoons *gochujang* (Korean fermented chile paste), divided

1 chipotle pepper in adobo sauce, finely chopped

1 tablespoons brown sugar

1½ teaspoons ground cumin

½ teaspoon ground coriander

1 teaspoon salt

1 cup dark beer

2 cups beef broth

One 15-ounce can diced tomatoes

½ cup sour cream

8 to 10 ounces mixed yellow and blue tortilla chips (about half a medium bag of each type)

¾ cup crumbled cotija cheese

2 serrano peppers, thinly sliced

DIRECTIONS

In a large saucepan or Dutch oven, heat 2 tablespoons of oil over high heat. Season the meat with salt and pepper. Working in batches, brown the meat all over, about 3 to 4 minutes; using a slotted spoon, transfer the meat to a paper towel–lined plate.

Add the remaining tablespoon of oil to the pan and heat over medium heat. Add the onion, garlic and jalapeño pepper and cook, stirring frequently, until softened, about 3 minutes. Add 6 tablespoons of *gochujang*, the chipotle pepper, sugar, cumin, coriander and salt; cook, stirring frequently, for 3 minutes. Add the beer, broth and tomatoes; using a wooden spoon, scrape up any browned bits on the bottom of the pot. Bring the chili to a simmer and cook until the meat is very tender, about 2 hours. Let the chili cool to room temperature and season to taste with salt. The chili can be made up to 1 day ahead.

In a small bowl, stir together the sour cream and remaining 2 teaspoons of gochujang.

Arrange the chips on a platter. Using a slotted spoon, scatter a layer of chili over the chips. Sprinkle the cotija cheese over the top. Dollop the *gochujang* sour cream over the cheese, garnish the nachos with the serrano peppers and serve.

"THIS RECIPE IS NOT FOR THE TIMID.

IT REQUIRES A LONG NIGHT, BEERS, WHISKEY AND LOUD MUSIC."

EAST BAY BURRITO NACHOS

MARIELLE & JORMA

Jorma Taccone, of the comedy trio The Lonely Island (*Popstar: Never Stop Never Stopping*) and writer-director Marielle Heller (*The Diary of a Teenage Girl*) both grew up in the East Bay of San Francisco, but didn't meet until they were in college at UCLA. The first time they were back home together, they headed out for a burrito, but fought about where to go. "We ended up at Ramiro and Sons, in Alameda, so I could convince him it's the best," says Heller. It only took her 15 years. "It hurts my heart to admit that I *might* like Ramiro more," says Taccone, a diehard fan of Gordo's in Berkeley. "My friends would kill me if they see that in print." So what makes an East Bay burrito so great? Simple ingredients, says Heller, whose brother, Nate, has been helping them perfect this nacho recipe in homage. To mimic the way the tortillas are steamed with cheese, they bake cheese slices on tostadas before layering on the burrito ingredients. Heller, a lifelong vegetarian, skips the carnitas and swears it's just as good. One important thing: "No fucking lettuce," says Jorma.

✦ ✦

INGREDIENTS

Makes 4 to 6 servings

For the carnitas:

3 pounds boneless, skinless pork shoulder

Strips of zest and juice from 1 orange

6 garlic cloves, smashed

1 large onion, diced

1 teaspoon crushed red pepper flakes

1 cinnamon stick

2 bay leaves

Kosher salt

For the guacamole:

1 avocado

¼ cup finely chopped white onion

2 teaspoons fresh lime juice

For the tostadas:

Twelve 6-inch corn tortillas

Vegetable oil

12 slices Monterey Jack cheese

1 can pinto beans, drained

Homemade Crema (page 141) or sour cream, for serving

½ cup Charred Salsa Verde (page 136), for serving

DIRECTIONS

Make the carnitas: Cut the pork into 1-inch cubes, discarding any large chunks of fat. Place the pork in a Dutch oven or large saucepan. Add enough water to cover the pork by 1 inch. Add the orange zest and juice, garlic, onion, red pepper flakes, cinnamon, bay leaves, 2 teaspoons of salt and the cloves. Bring the water to a boil, then reduce to a simmer. Skim off any foam that forms on the surface. Simmer the pork, uncovered and stirring occasionally, until very tender, about 1½ hours, adding small amounts of water if necessary to keep the meat submerged. Discard the orange zest, bay leaves and cinnamon. Continue cooking the pork until all of the liquid has evaporated. Increase the heat to high and fry the pork until crispy, about 10 minutes. Transfer to a plate and set aside.

Meanwhile, make the guacamole: Halve and pit the avocado and scoop the flesh into a bowl. Mash the avocado with a fork and stir in the onion and lime juice; season to taste with salt. Cover the bowl with plastic, pressing it onto the surface of the guacamole to prevent browning. Refrigerate until ready to use.

Make the tostadas: Preheat the oven to 400°F. Brush both sides of the tortillas with oil and sprinkle with salt. Arrange the tortillas in a single layer on a baking sheet. Bake until the tortillas are crisp and the edges are golden, about 15 minutes. Remove from the oven and set aside.

Arrange the tostadas on a large rimmed baking sheet. Place 1 slice of cheese on top of each tostada. Spoon some of the carnitas over the tostadas, followed by the pinto beans. Bake until the cheese has melted and the edges of the tostadas are starting to brown, 8 to 10 minutes. Remove from the oven and spoon the guacamole, salsa verde and crema over the top. Serve immediately.

"EAST BAY BURRITOS ARE THE PERFECT MEAL," SAYS HELLER. "IT'S ALL ABOUT GETTING **THE RIGHT BALANCE OF INGREDIENTS**," ADDS TACCONE.

"AND NO F*CKING LETTUCE."

INDIAN-STYLE LAMB NACHOS

CHRIS SHEPHERD

For this addictively spicy-savory recipe, Chris Shepherd, the chef and owner of Houston's widely celebrated restaurant Underbelly, took inspiration from the Indian street snack *pani puri*. "It's an homage to the Indian culture here in Houston," he says. "I first served these nachos at a food festival, and they were such a hit that they've become a regular on the menu at my house."

✦ ✦

INGREDIENTS

Makes 6 to 8 servings

1 tablespoon vegetable oil

1½ pounds ground lamb

1 medium onion, diced

1 tablespoon finely chopped fresh ginger

1 large garlic clove, finely chopped

1½ teaspoons ground cinnamon

¼ teaspoon ground nutmeg

1 teaspoon freshly ground black pepper

1 teaspoon ground fennel seeds

1 teaspoon cayenne pepper

¾ teaspoon ground cumin

1 tablespoon ground turmeric

1 tablespoon kosher salt

1 teaspoons unseasoned rice vinegar

1 cup labne (strained Greek yogurt) or fromage blanc

Zest and juice of 1 lime

30 *pani puri* shells (available at Indian markets)

½ cup Pickled Red Onion (page 142)

¼ cup chopped cilantro

DIRECTIONS

In a large skillet, heat the oil over medium-high heat. Add the lamb and cook, breaking the meat up with a wooden spoon, until the fat begins to render, about 5 minutes. Add the onion, ginger and garlic and cook, stirring, until the meat is almost cooked through and the vegetables have softened, about 5 minutes. Add the spices, salt and vinegar, lower the heat to medium low and cook, stirring occasionally, for 5 minutes longer.

In a bowl, blend the labne with the lime zest and juice.

Crack a hole in the top of each *pani puri* shell. Spoon some of the lamb mixture and a dollop of the labne into each shell. Top each with onion and cilantro and serve.

ULTIMATE ASIAN NACHOS

Meat-centric chef Naomi Pomeroy makes these nachos at Expatriate in Portland, Oregon. "I try to make the food there fun—nothing authentic," says Pomeroy. "These nachos were my take on stoner-ish food." The late, great food writer Josh Ozersky originally published the recipe in *Esquire*, calling these "maybe the best nachos in the world." Thanks to the combination of Asian flavors (lemongrass, ginger, hoisin, fish sauce, Thai chiles, kefir lime leaves) and a not-timid amount of Velveeta, we agree. As Pomeroy recalls, Ozersky requested these nachos at his Portland housewarming party, and Pomeroy complied. In fact, they are her go-to potluck dish as well. (Unlike most nachos, these travel well, as long as you keep the components separate until ready to serve.)

✦ ✦

INGREDIENTS

Makes 4 to 6 servings

For the meat:

2 pounds 80% lean ground beef

4 lemongrass stalks, white parts finely chopped

One 2-inch piece ginger, grated

6 garlic cloves, finely chopped

⅓ cup hoisin sauce

¼ cup Szechuan hot pot sauce

4 to 6 Thai bird's eye chiles

Kosher salt

For the queso:

One 10-ounce package Velveeta cheese, cut into 2-inch cubes

2 cups sour cream

8 to 12 Thai bird's eye chiles

For the salsa:

3 diced Roma tomatoes

¼ diced yellow onion

3 Thai bird's eye chiles, finely chopped

2 tablespoons Thai sweet chile sauce

1 tablespoon fish sauce

2 teaspoons rice wine vinegar

¾ teaspoon kosher salt

Spiced Wonton Chips (page 125)

1 cup Homemade Crema (page 141)

½ cup chopped cilantro

DIRECTIONS

Prepare the meat: In a large skillet, cook the meat over medium-high heat until well browned, about 8 minutes. Transfer the meat to a bowl and discard about half of the fat in the skillet. Add the lemongrass, ginger and garlic to the skillet and cook over medium heat, stirring frequently, until softened and fragrant, about 5 minutes. Add the hoisin, hot pot sauce and chiles and cook, stirring, for 3 minutes. Return the meat to the skillet and cook for 2 minutes longer. Season to taste with salt.

Make the queso: Set a mixing bowl or double boiler over simmering water and add the Velveeta, sour cream and chiles. Cook, stirring, until the cheese has melted. Keep warm until ready to use.

Make the salsa: In a bowl, toss all ingredients, refrigerate for about 30 minutes to allow the flavors to develop. Before using, strain the salsa through a fine-mesh strainer to remove most of the liquid

Assemble the nachos: Preheat the oven to 225°. Scatter the wonton chips on a baking sheet and bake until warmed through, 3 to 5 minutes (don't let the chips brown). Arrange half of the chips on a serving platter and top with some of the meat, queso, salsa, crema and cilantro. Repeat to make a second layer and serve.

"THESE NACHOS ARE MY TAKE ON **STONER-ISH FOOD.**"

SHREDDED PORK NACHOS
WITH PARSLEY SAUCE & FONTINA

Michael Schwartz and his stellar restaurant group (which includes Miami's fantastic Michael's Genuine Food & Drink, Harry's Pizzeria and Cypress Tavern) is known for the kind of simple, satisfying, fresh food you want to eat. A perfect example? These salty, savory, pork-laden nachos. "Balance is super important when I put together a dish," says Schwartz. "Nachos are no exception!"

✦ ✦

INGREDIENTS

Makes 4 to 6 servings

For the parsley sauce:

1 cup packed parsley leaves

3 tablespoons capers, rinsed and drained

2 oil-packed anchovies, drained

3 garlic cloves, coarsely chopped

½ teaspoon freshly ground black pepper

½ cup extra-virgin olive oil

For the nachos:

12 to 16 ounces white corn tortilla chips (1 large bag)

3 cups shredded roast pork

3 cups coarsely grated Fontina cheese

1 cup Pickled Red Onion (page 142)

3 serrano peppers, seeded and finely chopped

2 avocados—halved, pitted and diced

DIRECTIONS

Make the parsley sauce: Combine all the ingredients in a blender and puree until the mixture is completely smooth and bright green. The sauce should be wet and slightly soupy in consistency. (Makes about ¾ cup.)

Assemble the nachos: Preheat the oven to 400°. Scatter a third of the chips on a rimmed baking sheet. Top with a third each of the shredded pork and the cheese. Repeat to make two more layers. Bake the nachos until the cheese melts but doesn't brown, about 5 minutes. Top the nachos with the onions, peppers and avocado. Drizzle with about ½ cup of the parsley sauce and serve.

"BALANCE IS SUPER IMPORTANT

WHEN I PUT TOGETHER A DISH.
NACHOS ARE NO EXCEPTION!"

SALTED CARAMEL
ICE CREAM NACHOS

The ice cream company Coolhaus is famous for its ice cream sandwiches, so it was only a matter of time before co-founder Natasha Case developed an ice cream nacho recipe. "We were playing with a lot of elevated junk food ideas," she says, "and the staff would occasionally hit the corner store for snacks. One day it was tortilla chips, and we dipped them in our salted caramel and salted chocolate ice creams. It was addictive and delish. When we tried it with cinnamon and sugar chips, we knew we had something insane."

INGREDIENTS

Makes 4 to 6 servings

1 cup heavy cream

1 tablespoon sugar

1 teaspoon vanilla extract

10 ounces Cinnamon and Sugar Tortilla Chips (page 125)

1 pint salted caramel ice cream

½ cup butterscotch chips

⅓ cup caramel sauce, warmed

DIRECTIONS

In the bowl of a stand mixer fitted with the whisk attachment, whip the cream at medium-high speed until it forms stiff peaks. Beat in the sugar and vanilla and mix for 1 minute.

Arrange the chips on a platter. Place a few scoops of ice cream over the chips. Top with dollops of whipped cream, scatter the butterscotch chips on top and drizzle with the caramel sauce. Serve immediately.

"WE'VE MADE A LOT OF ELEVATED JUNK FOOD SUNDAES OVER THE YEARS,

BUT THIS ONE WAS THE BEST.

INSANELY ADDICTIVE."

PALMIER NACHOS
WITH SALTY BANANAS FLAMBÉ

We're not blowing smoke up his ass when we call Dominique Ansel a pastry genius. Ansel's obituary will probably mention the cronut—which birthed a nationwide craze—but the hybrid croissant-doughnut is just one of many examples of Ansel's brilliance. (His NYC bakery is constantly rolling out new inventions, such as chocolate chip cookie shots of milk.) Our favorite? These crispy-sweet nachos: homemade palmiers layered with bubbling salty-sweet bananas and crunchy hazelnuts. "We are constantly testing the boundaries of creativity," Ansel says. "But we never forget that the best desserts in the world are simply the ones that make you smile. And being able to eat with your hands is always a good thing."

INGREDIENTS

Makes 8 to 10 servings

1 sheet puff pastry, thawed if frozen
¼ cup turbinado sugar
2 tablespoons ground cinnamon
1 cup heavy cream
¼ cup granulated sugar
1 vanilla bean, split and seeds scraped
8 tablespoons (1 stick) salted butter
1 cup brown sugar
3 bananas, sliced into ½-inch rounds
¼ cup dark rum
3 tablespoons crushed hazelnuts, toasted
1 large pinch flaky sea salt

DIRECTIONS

Make the palmiers: Roll out the puff pastry to an even thickness of ¼ inch. Combine the turbinado sugar and cinnamon and sprinkle ¼ cup of the mixture evenly over the dough. Using a rolling pin, roll over the pastry lightly. Fold both sides of the dough into the center so they meet in the middle of the sheet. Sprinkle 1 tablespoon of the cinnamon sugar over the dough. Roll over the dough again to lightly press the sugar into the dough. Fold the left side over the right side, creating a long log of dough. Cover the dough with plastic wrap and refrigerate for 20 minutes.

Preheat the oven to 425°. Remove the dough from the refrigerator and slice it crosswise into ¾-inch discs. Transfer the cookies to a parchment paper–lined baking sheet, laying them cut-side up and several inches apart. Sprinkle the cookies with the remaining cinnamon sugar. Using a rolling pin, roll the cookies as thin as possible. Let rest for 30 minutes, then bake for 18 to 20 minutes, or until the palmiers are golden brown. Remove them from the oven and let cool.

In a large bowl (or using an electric stand mixer), beat the cream with the granulated sugar until stiff peaks form. Beat in the vanilla seeds and refrigerate until ready to use.

In a skillet, melt the butter over medium heat. Add the brown sugar and cook until bubbling, about 3 minutes. Add the bananas and cook, stirring and turning them occasionally, for 3 minutes. Remove the skillet from the heat and add the rum. Carefully light the rum on fire and let the flames subside. Return the skillet to the heat and cook for 2 minutes longer.

Arrange the palmiers on a serving platter in a single layer. Spoon the bananas flambé over the palmiers, filling in the gaps between the cookies. Dot the whipped cream over the palmiers, sprinkle with the hazelnuts and sea salt and serve immediately.

"NEVER FORGET THAT THE BEST DESSERTS IN THE WORLD ARE SIMPLY THE ONES THAT MAKE YOU SMILE. AND BEING ABLE TO EAT WITH YOUR HANDS IS ALWAYS A GOOD THING."

THE NACHO PANTRY

HOMEMADE TORTILLA CHIPS (FRIED)

INGREDIENTS

Makes 10 to 12 ounces

Twelve 6-inch corn tortillas

Vegetable or peanut oil, for frying

Kosher salt

DIRECTIONS

Cut each tortilla into 6 wedges. Heat 1 to 2 inches of oil in a Dutch oven, wok or large saucepan over medium-high heat until it reaches 375° on a deep-fry thermometer (adjust the flame as needed to maintain this temperature).

Working in batches of about 10 at a time, fry the tortilla wedges, agitating them with a metal strainer, until their edges just begin to brown, about 1 minute. Flip the chips over and continue frying until crisp and light golden brown, about 1 minute longer. Transfer the chips to a paper towel–lined tray, sprinkle with salt to taste, and let sit for 2 to 3 minutes to drain. Repeat with the remaining tortillas, checking the oil temperature between batches. Use right away or let cool to room temperature and store in a covered container for up to 1 day.

HOMEMADE TORTILLA CHIPS (BAKED)

INGREDIENTS

Makes 10 to 12 ounces

Twelve 6-inch corn tortillas

Vegetable oil

Kosher salt

DIRECTIONS

Position a rack in the center of the oven and preheat the oven to 400°. Use a pastry brush to generously coat the tortillas with oil. Cut each tortilla into 6 wedges. Arrange the tortillas in a single layer on a rimmed baking sheet and season generously with salt.

Bake the tortillas until golden brown and sizzling, about 7 minutes. Rotate the pan and bake until the chips are crisp and golden brown, about 5 minutes longer. Use right away or let cool to room temperature and store in a covered container for up to 1 day.

SPICED WONTON CHIPS

INGREDIENTS

Makes 4 dozen chips

1 tablespoon kosher salt

¼ teaspoon ground Szechuan peppercorns

¼ teaspoon ground cumin

¼ teaspoon ground coriander

24 square (thin) wonton skins

Neutral oil, such as canola or peanut, for frying

DIRECTIONS

In a small bowl, combine the salt, peppercorns, cumin and coriander. Set aside.

Add about 2 inches of oil to a medium heavy-bottomed saucepan or Dutch oven and heat the oil until it reaches 350° on a deep-fry thermometer.

Cut the wonton skins diagonally into triangles. Working in batches of about 10, separate the skins and fry them in the hot oil, agitating them with a fine-mesh strainer or spider as they fry. (Try to maintain an even temperature; the skins will darken too quickly if the oil becomes too hot.) When the wontons are crisp and golden brown, transfer them to paper towels to drain. Repeat until all of the chips are fried, then season the chips with the spice mix.

CINNAMON-SUGAR TORTILLA CHIPS

INGREDIENTS

Makes 10 to 12 ounces

¼ cup sugar

1 teaspoon ground cinnamon

Twelve 6-inch corn tortillas

Vegetable or peanut oil, for frying

DIRECTIONS

In a small bowl, combine the cinnamon and sugar and set aside. Cut each tortilla into 6 wedges. Heat 1 to 2 inches of oil in a Dutch oven, wok or large saucepan over medium-high heat until it reaches 375° on a deep-fry thermometer (adjust the flame as needed to maintain this temperature).

Working in batches of about 10 at a time, fry the tortilla wedges, agitating them with a metal strainer, until their edges just begin to brown, about 1 minute. Flip the chips over and continue frying until crisp and light golden brown, about 1 minute longer. Transfer the chips to a paper towel–lined tray, sprinkle generously with the cinnamon sugar, and let sit for 2 to 3 minutes to drain. Repeat with the remaining tortillas, checking the oil temperature between batches. Use right away or let cool to room temperature and store in a covered container up to 1 day.

FAUX-TEL
(OKLAHOMA-STYLE QUESO)

BILL HADER

Before acting on *Saturday Night Live* for eight seasons, starring in movies such as *Superbad* and *The Skeleton Twins*, and co-creating the show *Documentary Now*, Bill Hader was a film-obsessed kid growing up in Tulsa, Oklahoma. There, in Tex-Mex country, every party included a bowl of Ro-Tel dip: Velveeta melted with a can of Ro-Tel tomatoes and peppers. Here, Hader has given the dip an upgrade with Havarti and cheddar cheeses (plus just enough Velveeta to keep it creamy) and fresh tomatoes marinated with lime and pickled jalapeños. He admits, though, that it's been awhile since he's tasted them. "I would love nothing more than to eat these nachos," Hader says. "But now I'm an L.A. actor douchebag with a trainer who calls me a 'fat fuck' all week. If you make these and enjoy them, please contact me to describe what they taste like in great detail. I only know what kale tastes like at this point."

INGREDIENTS

Makes about 3 cups

3 medium tomatoes, diced

½ cup pickled jalapeño slices (from a jar or homemade; see page 142), diced

Juice of half a lime

¼ teaspoon salt

½ cup heavy cream

2 ounces Velveeta cheese, diced

8 ounces cheddar cheese, coarsely grated (2 cups)

8 ounces Havarti cheese, coarsely grated (2 cups)

DIRECTIONS

In a bowl, combine the tomatoes, jalapeño, lime juice and salt. Let sit for at least 10 minutes.

Meanwhile, in a medium saucepan, heat the cream over medium heat until it begins to steam. Add the Velveeta and stir until it's melted. Add the cheddar and Havarti and whisk the mixture until the cheese has melted and the sauce is smooth. Add the tomato-jalapeño mixture (don't drain) and stir until smooth. Keep warm until ready to use.

"IF YOU MAKE THESE AND ENJOY THEM, **PLEASE CONTACT ME** TO DESCRIBE WHAT THEY TASTE LIKE IN GREAT DETAIL. I ONLY KNOW WHAT **KALE** TASTES LIKE AT THIS POINT."

QUESO BLANCO

The chef at NYC's Birds & Bubbles and Rise Bakeshop in Columbia, South Carolina, Sarah Simmons comes from a town with so few dining options that her first memory of Mexican food was at a "fiesta" at the country club—and it was as horrible as you can imagine. "When a Mexican restaurant finally opened in my small South Carolina town, I remember that first scoop of white, creamy queso with herbaceous salsa like it was yesterday. I was sold. No matter what other toppings nachos have—pulled pork, ground beef, shaved chicken—they aren't nachos to me unless they are covered in this white queso dip."

INGREDIENTS

Makes about 2 cups

1 tablespoon canola oil

1 medium yellow onion, finely chopped

1 garlic clove, finely chopped

¼ cup heavy cream

¼ cup whole milk

12 ounces white American cheese (not processed), cubed

One 5-ounce cans diced green chiles, with liquid

2 jalapeño peppers, seeded and finely chopped

Kosher salt

DIRECTIONS

In a large saucepan, heat the oil over medium heat. Add the onion and cook until softened, about 5 minutes. Add the garlic and cook until fragrant, about 1 minute.

Add the cream and milk to the pan and lower the heat to medium low. When the milk begins to steam, stir in the cheese, a few cubes at a time, until it's melted. Stir in the chiles and jalapeños. Season to taste with salt and serve.

"NO MATTER WHAT OTHER TOPPINGS YOU USE
—PULLED PORK, GROUND BEEF, SHAVED CHICKEN—
NACHOS AREN'T NACHOS TO ME UNLESS THEY ARE COVERED IN
THIS WHITE QUESO DIP."

CREOLE QUESO

INGREDIENTS

Makes about 2 cups

6 tablespoons unsalted butter

6 tablespoons all-purpose flour

2 cups whole milk

3 ounces Monterey Jack cheese, coarsely grated (1 cup)

1 tablespoon Creole spice blend

DIRECTIONS

In a medium saucepan, melt the butter over low heat. Whisk in the flour and cook, whisking constantly, for 3 minutes. Turn the heat to high and whisk in the milk. Bring the mixture to a boil while whisking, then lower the heat and gently simmer, whisking occasionally, until thickened, about 5 to 7 minutes. Remove the pan from the heat, add the cheese and whisk the queso until it's smooth. Whisk in the Creole seasoning and keep warm until ready to use.

IDIAZABAL QUESO

INGREDIENTS

Makes about 2 cups

2 cups chicken broth, vegetable broth or milk

9 ounces Idiazabal cheese, grated (2¼ cups)

Salt and freshly ground black pepper

DIRECTIONS

In a saucepan, bring the broth to a simmer. Transfer to a blender and turn the blender to high power. Slowly add the cheese through the top of the blender and blend until emulsified. Season to taste with salt and pepper. Transfer the cheese to a saucepan and keep warm until ready to use.

CASHEW QUESO

INGREDIENTS

Makes 2 cups

8 ounces raw cashews

4 cups water

1 garlic clove

1 tablespoon ground turmeric

¾ cup nutritional yeast

2 tablespoons cider vinegar

1 tablespoon salt

DIRECTIONS

Place the cashews in a heatproof bowl. In a saucepan, bring the water to a boil and pour it over the cashews. Let the cashews soak for 15 minutes, then drain; reserve the soaking liquid.

In a high-powered blender, combine the cashews, garlic, turmeric, yeast, vinegar and salt. Add 2 cups of the soaking liquid. Blend until very smooth, about 2 minutes, thinning with more water if needed (the sauce should have the texture of melted cheese).

ANIMAL QUESO

INGREDIENTS

Makes about 3 cups

1⅓ cups half-and-half

4 ounces Velveeta cheese, diced

4 ounces Monterey Jack cheese, grated (1 cup)

4 ounces cheddar cheese, grated (1 cup)

2 chipotles in adobo sauce, chopped

2 teaspoons kosher salt

1 tablespoon chili or taco spice blend

DIRECTIONS

In a saucepan, bring the half-and-half and Velveeta to a simmer over medium heat, stirring until the Velveeta has melted, about 5 minutes. Whisk in the other cheeses until they're melted and smooth. Whisk in the chipotles, salt and spice blend and keep warm until ready to use.

BUTTERMILK QUESO

INGREDIENTS

Makes 1 cup

2 tablespoons extra-virgin olive oil, divided

1 garlic clove, finely chopped

1 shallot, finely chopped

¾ cups buttermilk, well shaken

1¼ cups finely grated aged cheddar cheese (4 ounces)

Salt and freshly ground black pepper

DIRECTIONS

In a small saucepan, warm 1 tablespoon of oil over medium heat. Add the garlic and shallot and cook until fragrant and slightly translucent, about 2 minutes. Turn off the heat and add the buttermilk and cheddar, stirring until the cheddar has melted.

Transfer the buttermilk-cheddar mixture to a blender and blend at medium speed while slowly drizzling in the remaining tablespoon of oil until the mixture is smooth. Season to taste with salt and pepper and keep warm until ready to use.

PROVOLONE QUESO

INGREDIENTS

Makes about 2 cups

1 cup heavy cream

1 teaspoon cornstarch

1½ cups shredded Provolone cheese

Kosher salt

DIRECTIONS

In a small saucepan, bring the cream and cornstarch to a simmer. Stir in the cheese until it's melted. Turn off the heat, season to taste with salt and keep warm until ready to use.

FOUR-CHEESE QUESO

INGREDIENTS

Makes about 2½ cups

¼ stick (4 tablespoons) unsalted butter

1 small yellow onion, thinly sliced

Kosher salt

⅓ cup all-purpose flour

2 cups whole milk

2 tablespoons Sriracha hot sauce

¼ cup grated mild cheddar cheese

¼ cup grated sharp cheddar cheese

2 tablespoons grated Parmesan cheese

2 tablespoons grated Asiago cheese

DIRECTIONS

In a large saucepan, melt the butter over medium-low heat. Add the onion and a pinch of salt and cook, stirring frequently, until the onion is very soft (don't let it brown), about 10 minutes. Add the flour and stir to coat the onion. Add the milk and Sriracha. Using an immersion blender, blend the onion into the milk until smooth. Bring the liquid to a simmer and cook for 4 minutes or until thick enough to coat the back of a spoon. Add the cheeses and blend until smooth. Season to taste with salt and more Sriracha, if desired. Keep warm until ready to use.

BASTION QUESO

INGREDIENTS

Makes 2 cups

1 cup whole milk

1 cup beer (nothing hoppy)

2 tablespoons pickled jalapeño brine

1 pound Velveeta Queso Blanco, shredded

DIRECTIONS

In a large saucepan, combine the milk, beer and jalapeño brine. Bring to a simmer over medium-high heat, then whisk in the Velveeta until it's melted and glossy. Keep warm until ready to use.

DOCTORED-UP BLACK-EYED PEAS

INGREDIENTS

Makes 2 cups

2 tablespoons extra-virgin olive oil

½ medium onion, cut into ¼-inch dice

1 garlic clove, finely chopped

1 teaspoon kosher salt

½ teaspoon each ground cumin, smoked paprika, chile powder and dried oregano

¼ teaspoon cayenne pepper

One 15-ounce can black-eyed peas, with liquid

DIRECTIONS

In a small saucepan, heat the oil over medium heat. Add the onion, garlic and salt and cook, stirring frequently, for 2 minutes. Add the cumin, paprika, chile powder, oregano and cayenne and stir well. Add the black-eye peas and liquid, bring to a simmer and cook, stirring occasionally, until thickened, about 15 minutes.

REFRIED BLACK BEANS (FROM A CAN)

INGREDIENTS

Makes about 2 cups

5 cups water, plus more as needed

1 dried avocado leaf (available at Mexican markets) or bay leaf

1 cup dried black beans

¼ cup canola oil

½ finely chopped Spanish onion

2 garlic cloves, minced

1 serrano chile, seeded finely chopped

1 tablespoon finely chopped epazote leaves (available at Mexican markets) or fresh oregano

Kosher salt

DIRECTIONS

In a medium saucepan, bring the water to a boil and add the avocado leaf. Add the beans, lower the heat and simmer until tender, about 1 hour, adding more water to keep the beans covered, if needed. Remove from the heat and set aside.

In a medium saucepan, heat the oil over medium heat. Add the onion, garlic, chile and epazote and cook, stirring, until the vegetables have softened, about 5 minutes. Add the black beans and their cooking liquid, season with 1 teaspoon of salt and cook until very tender, stirring frequently and adding more water as needed to keep the beans from drying out, 20 to 30 minutes. Using a wooden spoon or potato masher, mash about half of the beans and continue cooking for 3 minutes longer. Remove from the heat and season to taste with salt.

REFRIED BLACK BEANS (FROM SCRATCH)

INGREDIENTS

Makes 2½ cups

½ cup grapeseed oil

One 15-ounce can black beans, with liquid

1 tablespoon garlic powder

1 tablespoon onion powder

1 tablespoon chili or taco spice blend

1 cup water

Kosher salt

DIRECTIONS

In a medium saucepan, heat the oil over high heat. Add the black beans and liquid and cook, stirring frequently, for 1 minute. Add the garlic powder, onion powder, spice blend and water. Continue cooking, stirring frequently and mashing the beans with a potato masher or whisk, until half of the beans are mashed, about 10 minutes. Season to taste with salt. The beans can be made up to 3 days ahead; refrigerate until ready to use.

RAW TOMATILLO SALSA

INGREDIENTS

Makes about 2 cups

1 pound tomatillos (about 5 medium)—husks removed, washed and quartered

½ small white onion, diced

1 large jalapeño pepper (with our without seeds), coarsely chopped

1 large garlic clove, chopped

1 tablespoon kosher salt

2 teaspoons sugar

DIRECTIONS

In a blender, combine the tomatillos, onion, jalapeño and garlic. Stir in the salt and sugar and refrigerate until ready to use, for up to 3 days.

DUNGENESS CRAB SALSA
WITH SERRANO CREMA & CRISPY TORTILLAS

The inspiration behind this recipe? "The freshness and vibrancy of seafood salsas combined with both my love for crab and my desire to eat anything on a tortilla chip," says Stuart Brioza, co-chef and co-owner with his wife, Nicole Krasinski, of San Francisco's edgy-cool restaurants State Bird Provisions and The Progress. "Even though I could eat this crab dip day or night, every day of my life, it's best during Dungeness crab season."

✦ ✦

INGREDIENTS

Makes 4 to 6 servings

1 live Dungeness crab (about 2 pounds)

1 quart vegetable or canola oil

8 corn tortillas

Kosher salt

2 Japanese cucumbers, peeled and sliced on the bias

4 French breakfast radishes, quartered from stem to tip

½ cup Tomato Vinaigrette (page 140)

2 tablespoons cilantro, picked

2 scallions, thinly sliced

2 tablespoons radish sprouts

¼ cup Serrano Crema (page 141)

1 tablespoon extra-virgin olive oil

Flaky sea salt and freshly ground black pepper

DIRECTIONS

Cook the crab: Bring a large pot of salted water to a boil and prepare an ice bath. Lower the crab into the pot until it's completely submerged. Cook at a gentle boil for 13 minutes, then transfer to the ice bath until cool.

Remove the flap above the belly and turn the crab belly-side down. Remove the back shell and drain any excess liquid. Scoop out the golden crab butter and reserve for another use (it's great blended with softened butter). Remove and discard any gills from the sides of the body. Twist off the legs and claws. Using scissors or a cracker, crack the shell of each leg and claw and remove the meat using your fingers or a small fork. To remove the body meat, press gently on the body until you crack through the cartilage. Pull the body sections apart and dig out the pockets of meat. Discard any shells. Cover and refrigerate the meat until ready to use.

Fry the tortillas: Add at least 1 inch of oil to a medium skillet and heat the oil until it reaches 350° on a deep-fry thermometer. Working in batches, fry the tortillas until they're golden brown and crispy, 3 to 5 minutes. Transfer to paper towels to drain and season with salt.

In a medium serving bowl, gently toss the crab, cucumbers, radishes and tomato vinaigrette until all of the ingredients are well coated. Garnish with the cilantro, scallions and radish sprouts. Spoon the crema over the top and drizzle with olive oil.

Season with flaky salt and pepper and serve the crab salsa with the fried tortillas on the side.

"I COULD EAT THIS CRAB DIP DAY OR NIGHT,

LIFE."

GREEN TOMATO PICO DE GALLO

INGREDIENTS

Makes about 2 cups

1 large green tomato (or 2 medium), cored and cut into ¼-inch dice

½ medium yellow onion, cut into ¼-inch dice

Juice of 1 lime

1 small serrano or jalapeño pepper, finely chopped

1½ teaspoons kosher salt

3 tablespoons chopped cilantro

DIRECTIONS

In a medium bowl, toss all ingredients until well incorporated. Let sit at least 15 minutes before serving. The pico de gallo can be refrigerated for up to 3 days.

CHARRED SALSA VERDE

INGREDIENTS

Makes about 2 cups

1½ pounds tomatillos (about 10 medium)—husks removed, washed and halved

1 medium white onion, halved

2 to 4 serrano or jalapeño peppers (based on your spice tolerance, remove seeds and ribs for less heat), halved

10 to 15 sprigs cilantro, tough lower stems discarded, divided

1 tablespoon vegetable oil

Kosher salt

DIRECTIONS

Adjust an oven rack to 4 inches below the broiler and preheat the broiler to high. Scatter the tomatillos, onion halves and peppers on a foil-lined rimmed baking sheet. Broil until they're charred and blackened on top and the tomatillos are completely tender, 6 to 12 minutes. Transfer the vegetables and any accumulated juices to a blender, food processor or the cup of an immersion blender. Add half of the cilantro. Pulse until a coarse puree is formed.

In a medium saucepan, heat the oil over high heat until shimmering. Pour the salsa into the hot oil all at once (it will steam and sputter). Immediately start stirring and cook, stirring, until the salsa is darkened and thick enough to coat the back of the spoon, about 3 minutes. Remove from the heat. Finely chop the remaining cilantro and stir it into the salsa. Season to taste with salt. Let cool, then serve. The salsa can be refrigerated for up to 5 days.

PICO DE GALLO

INGREDIENTS

Makes 2 cups

1 cup diced tomatoes (about 1 large or 2 medium tomatoes)

¼ cup red onion, diced

1 jalapeño, seeded and finely chopped

¼ cup finely chopped cilantro

Juice of 1 lime

2 teaspoons olive oil

¼ teaspoon dried Mexican oregano

Salt to taste

DIRECTIONS

In a medium bowl, combine all the ingredients and mix well. Season to taste with salt. The pico de gallo can be refrigerated for up to 3 days.

SEVEN-PEPPER SALSA

INGREDIENTS

Makes about 3 cups

5 dried ancho chiles

3 dried pasilla negre chiles

1 poblano pepper

2 jalapeño peppers

1 habanero pepper

1 red bell pepper

6 Roma tomatoes, halved lengthwise

1 teaspoon canola oil

3 dried arbol chiles

1 tablespoons cumin seed, toasted and ground

3 garlic cloves, finely chopped

Juice of 1 lime

Salt

½ cup finely chopped cilantro

DIRECTIONS

Bring a medium saucepan of water to a boil. Turn off the heat and add the ancho and pasilla negre chiles. Leave the chiles in the water for 10 minutes, then transfer them to a cutting board. When the chiles are cool enough to handle, remove the stems and seeds.

Meanwhile, preheat the broiler and line a rimmed baking sheet with foil. Arrange the poblano, jalapeño and habanero peppers on the baking sheet and broil about 4 inches from the heat, turning frequently, until charred all over (remove the peppers as they are blackened and transfer to a bowl; the smaller ones will be done first). When all of the peppers are charred, cover the bowl with plastic wrap and let steam for 10 minutes. When the peppers are cool enough to handle, peel and seed them.

While the peppers steam, place the tomatoes, cut-side down, on the same baking sheet and broil until charred all over, about 5 to 7 minutes. When the tomatoes are cool enough to handle, peel and core them.

In a small saucepan, heat the oil over medium-high heat. Add the arbol chiles and toast until fragrant, about 10 to 15 seconds. Transfer to a cutting board and, when the chiles are cool enough to handle, remove the stems and seeds.

In a food processor, combine the roasted peppers, reconstituted chiles, toasted arbol chiles, cumin, garlic and lime juice. Pulse until smooth. Season to taste with salt, add the cilantro and pulse until combined. Refrigerate until ready to use; the salsa will taste its best after resting for a day or so.

AVOCADO-TOMATILLO SALSA

INGREDIENTS

Makes 3 cups

½ pound tomatillos (about 3 medium)—husked, washed and quartered

2 to 3 jalapeño or serrano peppers, seeded and chopped

1 small onion, chopped

2 garlic cloves, smashed

3 tablespoons cilantro leaves

Kosher salt

Juice of 1 lime

1 avocado, halved and pitted

DIRECTIONS

In the bowl of a food processor (or large mortar and pestle), combine the tomatillos, peppers, onion, garlic, cilantro and 1 teaspoon of salt. Pulse until a chunky paste forms (don't over-puree). Transfer the mixture to a bowl and add the lime juice. Fold in the avocado with a stiff whisk, mashing it as you go. Season to taste with salt.

GREEN CHILE SALSA

INGREDIENTS

Makes about 2 cups

5 Anaheim or Cubanelle peppers

2 jalapeño peppers

1 medium Spanish onion, cut into ¼-inch rings

3 garlic cloves, peeled

1 teaspoon cumin seeds

1 teaspoon coriander seeds

½ teaspoon brown mustard seeds

½ teaspoon ground cinnamon

½ teaspoon dried thyme

2 allspice berries

½ cup cider vinegar

½ cup distilled white vinegar

½ cup cilantro leaves

½ cup water

Kosher salt

1 cup homemade aioli (preferable) or store-bought mayonnaise

DIRECTIONS

Preheat the broiler and line a rimmed baking sheet with foil. Arrange the peppers, onion and garlic on the baking sheet and broil about 4 inches from the heat, turning frequently, until charred all over, removing the ingredients as they're finished (the onion and garlic will be done before the peppers). Transfer the peppers to a bowl, cover with plastic wrap and let steam for 10 minutes. When they're cool enough to handle, peel and seed the peppers.

Meanwhile, toast the spices in a skillet over medium heat until fragrant, about 3 minutes. Finely grind the spices in spice grinder or with a mortar and pestle.

In a food processor, combine the peppers, onion, garlic, vinegars, cilantro, spices and water. Process until smooth, then season to taste with salt.

In a bowl, combine about 1 cup of the chile puree with the aioli, adding more chile puree if desired. The sauce can be covered and refrigerated for up to 3 days.

CLASSIC GUACAMOLE

INGREDIENTS

Makes about 2 cups

2 avocados, halved and pitted

1 tablespoon fresh lime juice, plus more to taste

2 tablespoons finely chopped white onion

1 garlic clove, finely grated

¼ cup finely chopped cilantro

Kosher salt

Pinch of cayenne pepper

DIRECTIONS

In a bowl, use a fork to lightly mash the avocados with the lime juice, leaving the avocado as chunky as you like. Stir in the onion, garlic, cilantro and cayenne. Season to taste with salt and more lime juice, if needed. Cover the surface with plastic wrap until ready to serve, up to 2 hours.

SMOKY GUACAMOLE

INGREDIENTS

Makes about 3 cups

3 avocados, halved and pitted

Juice of half a lime, plus more to taste

½ medium red onion, finely chopped

2 plum tomatoes—cored, seeded and diced

1½ tablespoons pureed canned chipotle peppers in adobo sauce

3 tablespoons chopped cilantro

Kosher salt

DIRECTIONS

In a bowl, use a fork to lightly mash the avocados with the lime juice, leaving the avocado as chunky as you like. Stir in the onion, tomatoes, chipotle puree and cilantro. Season to taste with salt and more lime juice, if needed. Cover the surface with plastic wrap until ready to serve, up to 2 hours.

ROMESCO SAUCE

INGREDIENTS

Makes 2 cups

¾ cup extra-virgin olive oil (preferably Spanish), divided

½ medium Spanish onion, thinly sliced

2 garlic cloves, smashed

1 small bell pepper, seeded and chopped

2 morita peppers (dried red jalapeños), chopped with seeds

3 Roma tomatoes, diced

⅓ cup toasted Marcona almonds

3 tablespoons red wine vinegar

Piment d'Espelette (Spanish chile powder)

DIRECTIONS

In a medium saucepan, heat ½ cup of oil over medium-low heat. Add the onion and cook until translucent, about 7 minutes. Add the garlic and cook until soft, about 2 minutes. Add the bell pepper and morita peppers, cover the pan and cook until the peppers are very tender, about 15 minutes. Add the tomatoes and almonds, cover the pot and cook over low heat until the tomatoes have completely broken down, about 45 minutes.

Transfer the contents of the pan to a blender or food processor and add the vinegar, the remaining oil and the Piment d'Espelette to taste. Blend until smooth. The romesco can be made ahead and refrigerated for up to 1 week.

BLACK HOT SAUCE

INGREDIENTS

Makes 1½ cups

1 small white onion, cut into ½-inch slices
1 large poblano pepper
3 jalapeño peppers
3 serrano peppers
3 habanero peppers
1 bulb roasted garlic, separated into cloves
1 tablespoon honey
Kosher salt, to taste

DIRECTIONS

Prepare a hot grill or preheat the broiler to high. Grill (or broil) the onion and peppers, turning frequently, until blackened all over, removing the smaller peppers as they're finished (the poblanos will take the longest). When the peppers are cool enough to handle, discard the stems and seeds (or leave the seeds in if you like a very spicy salsa). Transfer the peppers to a blender, add the garlic and honey and blend at high speed until the sauce is smooth; season to taste with salt. Refrigerate until ready to use, for up to 1 week.

SPICY PIZZA SHOP VINAIGRETTE

INGREDIENTS

Makes about ¼ cup

2 tablespoons red wine vinegar
3 tablespoons extra-virgin olive
1 garlic clove, smashed
1 teaspoon crushed red pepper flakes
½ teaspoon dried oregano
½ teaspoon freshly ground black pepper
Kosher salt

DIRECTIONS

Combine all ingredients in a blender and blend until smooth. Season to taste with salt.

TOMATO VINAIGRETTE

INGREDIENTS

Makes about 1 cup

1 cup canned whole peeled tomatoes
1 tablespoon fresh lime juice
1 teaspoon kosher salt
½ garlic clove, finely grated
1 dash Tabasco hot sauce
¼ small jalapeño pepper, seeded and finely grated

DIRECTIONS

Combine all the ingredients in a blender. Blend at medium-low speed until almost smooth (the tomato seeds should still be whole). Pass the mixture through a fine-mesh sieve into a bowl, pressing on the solids with a spoon. Discard the solids. Cover the vinaigrette and refrigerate until ready to use, for up to 1 day.

HOMEMADE CREMA

INGREDIENTS

Makes 2 cups

1 cup sour cream

1 cup heavy cream

1 teaspoon kosher salt

Fresh lime juice, optional

DIRECTIONS

In a bowl, whisk together the sour cream, heavy cream and salt. Cover the bowl and let the mixture sit at room temperature for at least 2 hours. The crema can be refrigerated until the same date as the expiration date for the sour cream or heavy cream. Bring the crema to room temperature before serving; season to taste with lime juice if desired.

SERRANO CREMA

INGREDIENTS

Makes about ½ cup

¼ ounce serrano pepper (about ½ a pepper), seeded

¼ cup buttermilk, shaken

1 teaspoon fresh lemon juice

1 teaspoon kosher salt

2½ tablespoons crème fraîche

DIRECTIONS

Finely chop the serrano or mash it onto a paste using a mortar and pestle.

In a small mixing bowl, whisk together the pepper, buttermilk, lemon juice and salt. Add the crème fraîche and whisk until smooth. Refrigerate until ready to use, for up to 2 days.

HARISSA AIOLI

INGREDIENTS

Makes about ¾ cup

½ cup mayonnaise

3 tablespoons harissa paste

3 tablespoons tomato paste

2 teaspoons sugar

2 teaspoons kosher salt

DIRECTIONS

In a small bowl, whisk together all ingredients until smooth. Refrigerate until ready to use, for up to 2 weeks.

RED PEPPER RELISH

INGREDIENTS

Makes 2 cups

4 red bell peppers, cored and thinly sliced

1 medium white onion, thinly sliced

4 garlic cloves, thinly sliced

1 cup cider vinegar

¼ teaspoon cayenne

½ teaspoon ground cumin

½ cup sugar

Juice of 1 lemon

Kosher salt

DIRECTIONS

In a large saucepan, combine the peppers, onion, garlic, vinegar, cayenne, cumin and sugar. Bring the mixture to a simmer and cook until the liquid has evaporated and the peppers are very tender, 15 to 20 minutes. Transfer to a food processor and pulse until the mixture is a relish-like consistency. Stir in the lemon juice and season to taste with salt. Cover and refrigerate until ready to use, for up to 1 week.

PICKLED JALAPEÑOS

INGREDIENTS

Makes 1 quart

8 to 12 jalapeño peppers (depending on size)

3 cups apple cider vinegar

2 tablespoons kosher salt

DIRECTIONS

Wash the peppers and place them in a quart Mason jar. In a saucepan, bring the vinegar and salt to a boil, then pour the mixture over the peppers. Seal the jar and let cool to room temperature, then refrigerate until ready to use, for up to 1 month.

PICKLED RED ONION

INGREDIENTS

Makes about ½ cup

½ cup red wine or cider vinegar

1 tablespoon sugar

1 teaspoon kosher salt

1 red onion, halved and thinly sliced

DIRECTIONS

In a Mason jar, combine the vinegar, sugar and salt. Seal the jar and shake until the salt and sugar have dissolved. Add the onion, seal the jar and shake again. Let sit at room temperature for 1 hour before using. Refrigerate until ready to use, for up to 1 week.

REFRESCOS

CLASSIC MARGARITA

The margarita's origin story—or at least one of several purported histories—is remarkably similar to that of nachos. In 1938, a Tijuana bartender named Carlos Herrera is said to have created the drink on the fly to satisfy the needs of a fussy American customer, this one an actress who was allergic to all spirits with the exception of tequila. We may never know the cocktail's true genesis, but we do know that its sweet-sour-salty personality has helped it become America's favorite cocktail to drink with food—especially nachos.

✦ ✦

INGREDIENTS

Makes 1 drink

2 lime wedges, 1 for the rim and 1 for garnish
Coarse salt
2 ounces blanco tequila
1 ounce Cointreau (or other triple sec)
1 ounce fresh lime juice
Lime wedge, for garnish (optional)

DIRECTIONS

Wet the rim of a cocktail glass with a lime wedge and rim with salt. Fill a cocktail shaker with ice and add the remaining ingredients. Shake well, then strain into the cocktail glass, garnish with a lime wedge (if using) and serve.

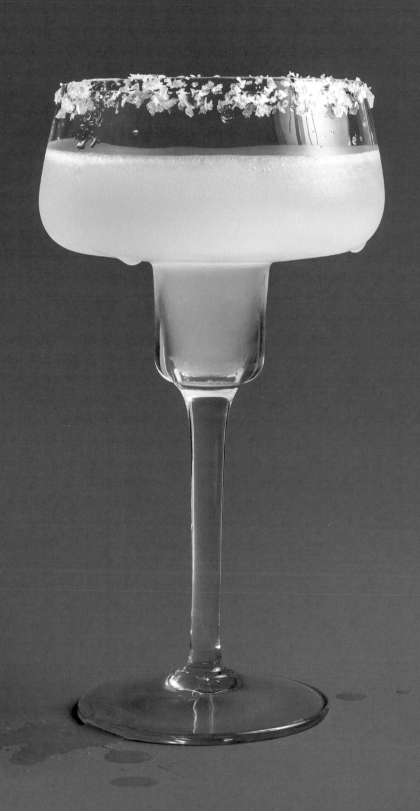

SPICY WATERMELON
MARGARITA

Though it might look pretty in pink, our spicy watermelon margarita has enough punch to take on any other margarita in the ring. Anyone whose drink preferences include "tequila" and "spicy" will love this cocktail. To make fresh watermelon juice, puree a few chunks of watermelon (no rinds, please) in a blender or food processor and pass through a fine-mesh strainer.

✦ ✦

INGREDIENTS

Makes 1 drink

2 thin slices jalapeño pepper, with seeds, plus 1 slice for garnish

1 ounce mezcal or tequila

1 ounce tequila

¾ ounce simple syrup

1 ounce fresh watermelon juice

¾ ounce fresh lime juice

Lime wheel, for garnish

DIRECTIONS

In a cocktail shaker, combine the jalapeño slices, mezcal, tequila, simple syrup, watermelon juice and lime juice. Shake well, then strain into a cocktail glass. Garnish with the lime wheel and remaining jalapeño slice and serve.

PALOMA

The margarita might rule over America's Mexican-restaurant menus, but south of the border, the paloma is king. There it's usually made by simply combining tequila and grapefruit soda (Mexico's answer to a rum and Coke), but our version is amped up with mezcal and fresh juice.

✦ ✦

INGREDIENTS

Makes 1 drink

Lime wedge

Coarse salt

2 ounces mezcal

2 ounces grapefruit juice

½ ounce fresh lime juice

2 to 3 ounces club soda

Lime twist, for garnish

DIRECTIONS

Wet the rim of a highball glass with a lime wedge and rim with salt. Fill the glass with ice cubes and add the mezcal, grapefruit juice and lime juice. Stir to combine the ingredients, then top with club soda. Garnish with a lime twist and serve.

SANGRITA

This spicy sidecar comes from tequila's birthplace in Jalisco, Mexico, and is meant to be served as a chaser alongside sipping (or shooting, if that's your speed) tequila or mezcal. Anyone who's discovered the magic of sangrita has come up with his or her own recipe, so consider ours a template upon which to build your own.

+ +

INGREDIENTS

Makes 2 to 4 drinks

4 ounces fresh orange juice

4 ounces tomato juice (preferably fresh, but canned is fine)

2 ounces fresh lime juice

Hot sauce, to taste

Pinch of salt

DIRECTIONS

Fill a cocktail shaker with ice and add the remaining ingredients. Shake well and strain into a short glass to serve alongside tequila or mezcal.

MICHELADA

Beer cocktails are often met with skepticism in America (beer over ice?!), but if you think of the Michelada as a beer-based bloody Mary, you'll find yourself raiding the pantry for the savory seasonings that make this both a food- and session-friendly drink.

INGREDIENTS

Makes 1 drink

1 teaspoon coarse salt

¼ teaspoon chile powder

1 lime wedge

¼ ounce Worcestershire sauce

¼ ounce Maggi or soy sauce

¼ ounce hot sauce, such as Tabasco or Cholula

¼ ounce fresh lime juice

12 ounces Mexican lager

Grape tomato and lime wheel, for garnish

DIRECTIONS

Combine the salt and chile powder on a plate. Wet the rim of a cocktail glass with a lime wedge and rim with the salt mixture. Fill a highball glass with ice cubes and add the Worcestershire, Maggi, hot sauce and lime juice. Stir to combine, then top with the beer, garnish with the tomato and lime wheel and serve.

MEXICAN BEER CHEAT SHEET

Nachos obviously call for beer, ideally a Mexican brand. Don't pick one at random, though. Here's how to tell your Coronas from your Modelos.

✦ ✦

DOS EQUIS AMBER

The amber Vienna-style lager is a better, more flavorful choice than the more pervasive (and more "meh") Dos Equis Special Lager.

PACIFICO

If you're looking for a lighter beer, this is a good option. Its malty, fruity notes give it more personality than most lagers, and the brown bottle means it won't be skunked.

CORONA

Fairly watery and bland on its own, but a generous squeeze of zippy lime makes it more gulpable. And those miniature Coronita bottles are dang cute.

NEGRA MODELO

Bottles of this dark, rich beer sit on restaurant and bar tables throughout Mexico (it's the best-selling dark beer in the country). Essentially a German-style dunkel, Negra Modelo is super flavorful yet lighter in body than the color would have you believe. If you're not a dark beer person, Modelo Especial and Modelo Light are decently flavorful options. But really, try the Negra Modelo.

TECATE

A mild, inoffensive (and mostly uninteresting) beer that's almost too easy to gulp down. Great for micheladas and chasing tequila-based drinks.

ABOUT THE AUTHOR

Gina Hamadey writes about travel and food for *Food & Wine*, *Travel + Leisure*, *Saveur* and *Wine Enthusiast*, among others. She is the editor of the quarterly magazine *Beekman 1802 Almanac*, and was previously travel editor at *Food & Wine* and *Rachael Ray Every Day* magazines.

DOVETAIL

Published by Dovetail Press in Brooklyn, New York, a division of Assembly Brands LLC.

For details or ordering information, contact the publisher at the address below or email **info@dovetail.press.**

Dovetail Press

42 West Street #403

Brooklyn, NY 11222

www.dovetail.press

Library of Congress Cataloging-in-Publication data is on file with the publisher.

ISBN: 978-0-9898882-3-3

First Edition

Printed in China

10 9 8 7 6 5 4 3 2 1